Praise for *Stronger Than the Struggle*

"I love Havilah. She is fierce and kind and in so many ways the little sister I never had, which is why I am thrilled she has taken the time to capture these truths in *Stronger Than the Struggle*. On these pages she demystifies and de-weirds the topic of spiritual warfare with a get-real approach that lends perspective while equipping you with practical tools. We wrestle not with flesh and blood, but it would be a mistake to imagine that we do not wrestle. The good news is that we don't do it alone and in Christ we win!"

—**Lisa Bevere**, *New York Times* bestselling author and cofounder Messenger International

"We are in a fight, we may not want it or acknowledge it, but that doesn't change the fact that we are in it. It's time we learned how to fight right, to take a hold of what God has given us and use the power that resides within us. This book will help you become stronger than your struggle."

—**Charlotte Gambill**, lead pastor of Life Church UK

"The struggle and the fight are not topics we like to talk much about in the church. If we do, we often approach it from a place of defeat rather than victory. As the popular saying goes, 'the struggle is real,' but God has prepared us with the necessary strength to walk in victory. I am grateful that Havilah has written so beautifully about the strength found in God for whatever struggle you may be facing. Not only is Havilah a dear friend, but she is one of my favorite Bible teachers. In a clear and brilliantly communicated manner, she brings the Word to life in a profound yet practical way. This same ability to communicate God's Word shines through in her writing. *Stronger Than the Struggle* is a book for anyone who wants to fully walk out the victory available in Jesus."

—**Banning Liebscher**, founder and pastor of Jesus Culture

"I love how Havilah approaches this topic with boldness and authenticity. She wholeheartedly lives this message, reminding us that we have everything in Christ we need to win."

—**Christine Caine**, bestselling author and founder of A21 and Propel Women

"Christian language like *warfare* or *supernatural battle* might feel scary or confusing. Overwhelming explanations of otherworldly occurrences can be difficult to understand! But Havilah has taken a difficult subject and made it simple. Y   fight and I love how Havilah has   how to use it!"

—**Bianca Olthof**   f *Play with Fire*

"Havilah Cunnington is an absolute treasure. She's one of the most gifted communicators I know. Her insights and stories, laced with fabulous humor, always have deep impact on me. And now she brings us this wonderful book, *Stronger Than the Struggle*. It is packed with wisdom and practical application of truths to help each of us succeed in a life that has conflict. This conflict is called spiritual warfare. There's no escaping the fact that battles exist, as we were born into this war. But they need not become our focus, nor should they become a place of discouragement. Here Havilah leads us into profound yet practical truths that inspire a heart of absolute trust in a good and perfect Father who always ensures our victory. I believe this book will become a source of encouragement and insight for countless numbers of people. Be one of them!"

— **Bill Johnson**, senior leader of Bethel Church and author of *When Heaven Invades Earth* and *God Is Good*

"Spiritual battles are often perceived as weird or mystical. Havilah brings great clarity to the subject and provides simple, relevant ways to address them in your life. *Stronger Than the Struggle* will revolutionize your faith walk and prepare you for whatever comes your way!"

— **John Bevere**, bestselling author and cofounder of Messenger International

"In Havilah's new book, *Stronger Than the Struggle*, her authoritative and down-to-earth perspective on spiritual warfare sheds light on the spirit realm in a way that is clear and easy to understand. I believe Havilah's story will dispel any fear that you may have when approaching the mysteries of the unseen realm. This book is a practical guide to spiritual warfare. Read this book and you will be equipped with tools to overcome the battles that all Christians face. *Stronger Than the Struggle* could very well change your life forever!"

— **Kris Vallotton**, senior associate leader of Bethel Church, cofounder of Bethel School of Supernatural Ministry, and author of *The Supernatural Ways of Royalty* and *Spirit Wars*

"I adore Havilah and her message that no matter what comes our way, because of Jesus we are stronger than the struggle. Havilah spotlights our real enemy and how to fight back in powerful yet practical ways. If you want to walk in strength and confidence, this book will give you tools to do just that!"

— **Alli Worthington**, author of *Fierce Faith*

"I am SUPER excited about this book so beautifully named *Stronger Than the Struggle*. Too often we tend to complicate life, which leads to more battles than necessary instead of living a life trusting that God's got everything under control. In this warfare manual, as I like to call it, we are given specific tools to discern, understand, and conquer once and for all! Your life will never be the same after reading this and you WILL become stronger than your struggle!"

—**Real Talk Kim**, author of *Beautifully Whole* and senior pastor at Church of the Harvest

"Havilah is my GIRL! I've known her for nineteen years and she is the real deal. Authentic, powerful, happy, in love with the Word of God, a loving wife and mom, a great friend, and a powerful communicator who speaks and writes the timely heart of God."

—**Jenn Johnson**, cofounder of Bethel Music

"This book carries a living word for each of us. Through her wisdom and life experiences, Havilah reveals divine insights that bring understanding to spiritual warfare, clarity to our identity, and purpose to the struggle."

—**Karen Wheaton**, founder and senior leader of the Ramp

"An invaluable, heartfelt, spiritual insight that will both encourage and excite the reader. This affirming message of spiritual warfare must be read and treasured."

—**Heather Lindsey**, speaker and author of *Silent Seasons*

"The spiritual struggle is real and often defined wrongly by the people who are supposed to lead us. I remember when I was learning my spiritual authority and going through some very real battles with insecurity, spiritual encounters, and even just flat out intimidation from the enemy. I was looking for a book like this. I have read so many books that didn't empower me but left me more confused. Along comes Havilah's book, *Stronger than the Struggle*. I am so glad she wrote it and I am so glad this generation has it because we are living in a time with the most emotionally intelligent people who need an emotionally intelligent writer to define from her own experience the struggle and the overcoming. Havilah holds no punches in her own vulnerability with struggles and spiritual battles. I felt myself in those pages as I read them and I know so many of you will too! Talk about a tool for clearly understanding the struggle and our place of authority in it! I think like me, you will be so grateful you had Havilah's life picture and stories along with her excellent teaching to draw a line in your heart over your very own spiritual journey and God's power through the scriptures to help you navigate."

—**Shawn Bolz**, television personality, minister, and author of *Translating God*, *God Secrets*, and *Growing Up with God*

"Part girl-next-door, part wise prophet, Havilah Cunnington is the kind of woman you want to both share dessert with and take notes from. Plus, every time I'm with her I feel like I've been treated by a spiritual audiologist because I walk away hearing God's voice more clearly! And I can pretty much guarantee you'll feel the same way after perusing the pages of her new book, *Stronger Than the Struggle*."

—**Lisa Harper**, author of *A Perfect Mess* and *Believing Jesus*

"We all have struggles. At times, they seem overwhelming. But what is truly rare, is someone who can articulate with everyday insights and practical ways to overcome these difficulties. Havilah has been given this gift. With humor and humility, she is able to guide us out of emotional dead ends. *Stronger Than the Struggle* will show you the way, where a moment ago, there seemed to be no way. I'm confident this message will speak to you!"

—**Francis Anfuso**, senior pastor at Rock of Roseville and preacher at KLove

"Havilah is one of my favorite storytellers. Her comedic timing is only matched by her ability to gently expose the human condition in all its grit and glory with a wink. At a time in history filled with relative truth, Havilah makes it her daily practice to search out the clearest, most liberating of all the 'truths.' She delivers it in a way that we feel an immense sense of not only clarity, but belonging and camaraderie. This book is bound to give us tools that we've been long looking for. Tools that will help us get free and stay free."

—**Amanda Cook**, singer/songwriter

"Havilah Cunnington has the ability to take complex scriptural truths, like spiritual warfare, and break them down into simple concepts that every believer is able to digest and apply to their lives practically. Throughout the pages of this book, Havilah equips you with the tools necessary to be victorious in Jesus against the very real battle happening for your souls here on earth."

—**Andi Andrew**, author of *She Is Free*, copastor of Liberty Church, and found of the She Is Free Conference

Stronger
THAN THE
STRUGGLE

Also by Havilah Cunnington

Radical Growth
The Good Stuff
The Naked Truth About Sexuality
Eat. Pray. Hustle.
Soul Food

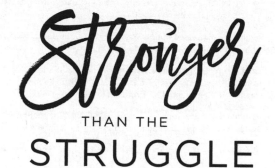

Stronger

THAN THE
STRUGGLE

UNCOMPLICATING YOUR
SPIRITUAL BATTLE

HAVILAH CUNNINGTON

NELSON
BOOKS

An Imprint of Thomas Nelson

Published in Nashville, Tennessee, by Nelson Books, an imprint of Thomas Nelson. Nelson Books and Thomas Nelson are registered trademarks of HarperCollins Christian Publishing, Inc.

The author is represented by Alive Literary Agency, 7680 Goddard Street, Suite 200, Colorado Springs, Colorado 80920, www.aliveliterary.com.

Thomas Nelson titles may be purchased in bulk for educational, business, fund-raising, or sales promotional use. For information, please e-mail SpecialMarkets@ThomasNelson.com.

Unless otherwise noted, Scripture quotations are taken from *The Message*. Copyright © by Eugene H. Peterson 1993, 1994, 1995, 1996, 2000, 2001, 2002. Used by permission of NavPress. All rights reserved. Represented by Tyndale House Publishers, Inc.

Scripture quotations marked AMP are from the Amplified® Bible. Copyright © 1954, 1958, 1962, 1964, 1965, 1987 by The Lockman Foundation. Used by permission. (www.Lockman.org)

Scripture quotations marked KJV are from the King James Version. Public domain.

Scripture quotations marked NIV are from the Holy Bible, New International Version®, NIV®. Copyright © 1973, 1978, 1984, 2011 by Biblica, Inc.® Used by permission of Zondervan. All rights reserved worldwide. www.Zondervan.com. The "NIV" and "New International Version" are trademarks registered in the United States Patent and Trademark Office by Biblica, Inc.®

Scripture quotations marked NKJV are from the New King James Version®. © 1982 by Thomas Nelson. Used by permission. All rights reserved.

Scripture quotations marked NLT are from the Holy Bible, New Living Translation. © 1996, 2004, 2007, 2013, 2015 by Tyndale House Foundation. Used by permission of Tyndale House Publishers, Inc., Carol Stream, Illinois 60188. All rights reserved.

Scripture quotations marked TPT are taken from *The Psalms: Poetry on Fire, The Passion Translation*TM, copyright © 2012. Used by permission of 5 Fold Media, LLC, Syracuse, NY 13039, United States of America. All rights reserved.

Any Internet addresses, phone numbers, or company or product information printed in this book are offered as a resource and are not intended in any way to be or to imply an endorsement by Thomas Nelson, nor does Thomas Nelson vouch for the existence, content, or services of these sites, phone numbers, companies, or products beyond the life of this book.

ISBN 978-0-7180-94218 (eBook)

Library of Congress Cataloging-in-Publication Data

ISBN 978-0-7180-94195
Names: Cunnington, Havilah, 1977- author.
Title: Stronger than the struggle : uncomplicating your spiritual battle /Havilah Cunnington.
Description: Nashville : Thomas Nelson, 2018.
Identifiers: LCCN 2017026627 I ISBN 9780718094195
Subjects: LCSH: Spiritual warfare.
Classification: LCC BV4509.5 .C86 2018 I DDC 235/.4--dc23 LC record available at https://lccn.loc.gov/2017026627

Printed in the United States of America

18 19 20 21 22 LSC 10 9 8 7 6

Dedicated to the five men in my life,
you've shown me what dreams look
like when they come true.

Contents

Foreword

I'll never forget the morning I met Havilah, a sunny February in Florida, four years ago.

I'd had a vivid dream just hours prior, which ended with a few key phrases that woke me up. Startled and shaken, I googled the peculiar phrases (yes, googled!) and somehow the internet took me down a rabbit trail to a specific passage of scripture.

Sleep was a lost cause at this point, so I eventually staggered into our morning meeting, words ringing loud, heavy of heart.

There were thirty women in attendance and wouldn't you know, I was assigned a seat next to this bright beauty named Havilah. Within minutes I knew I could trust her. A chronic over-sharer the bulk of my life, I went for it. I verbally vomited my experience from the night before.

Here's where we need to pause. I don't recommend starting new friendships sharing literal dreams. It will likely send them running. Turns out this was the exact right thing to do with a girl like Havilah. I determined our exchange that morning sealed our friendship forever, whether or not she knew it. Looking back, I know God gave me that dream and provided an immediate resource in Havilah. In the creation story, a river flowed out of Eden into the land of Havilah, rich in gold. Life-giving words that mine for gold, that's the person she's been to so many.

These pages aren't self-help, how-to, or tips to live a better life. No. This book is a rescue manual, to "punch the enemy in the throat in Jesus' name" and help others do the same.

Too much? Indeed. I don't think Jesus would have it any other way. The cross wasn't optional, insignificant, or irrelevant. The cross was imperative for the life-giving power of God to flow through our veins. Resurrection life.

The reason many of our peers left the church upon becoming adults isn't because there weren't well-intentioned hearts, it's because these dear ones never experienced a God of power.

I decided to follow Jesus at age five, but it wasn't until age thirty-seven that the Spirit of God arrested my life. I'd suffered panic disorder for almost two years in New York City before that fateful night I found words that were not my own. "Rescue me. Deliver Me. I cannot do this without you."

The panic immediately ceased under the weight of God's glory. Here's what I've learned: when you're sick you only see inward; when healing begins you see everyone else.

I immediately began to notice fear all around, people

walking through struggle, needing someone to tell them their story isn't over.

Perhaps you're picking up this book and haven't been taught to comprehend the resources of heaven brought to us by Holy Spirit. That was me.

Scripture tells us to work out our faith with fear and trembling. We often critique what we cannot understand, so I ask you this. Read these pages with hearts wide open. Before each chapter, ask God to break off any barriers of doubt, control, or cynicism.

We cannot be the people of God and declare we understand the mysteries of God. We stand in reverential awe. The only thing God makes certain to us is his nature. That's all we need, to believe. His means and methods are up to his discretion.

The ways in which God draws us close, softens our hearts, turns unbelief to belief, are vast and mysterious. We need only to trust him. His heart intent is always to bring us back to life.

If you've wandered the wilderness for as long as you can remember, I pray these pages fan a flame in your heart. There's more freedom waiting.

It's time to come home.

Rebekah Lyons, author of
Freefall to Fly and *You are Free*

Chapter 1

Spiritual Warfare
in Real Life

I grew up knowing my best was not good enough, that I was a dreadfully insignificant girl at the end of a long line of overachieving, brilliant, highly educated people I called family. My grandfather was an Italian immigrant who, at the age of six, took the long boat ride with his family to Ellis Island in New York City, hoping for a better life. He shined shoes as a boy and worked his way up to being a successful attorney, a five-term US congressman, and eventually a Supreme Court justice in New York State.

The same drive to succeed was deeply embedded in his highly motivated sons, who migrated to the West Coast after giving their lives to Christ and beginning new chapters of their lives in pursuit of Jesus. Even with their change of scenery and occupation, success followed close behind. They started evangelistic movements and ministries that reached a large part of the church nationwide. They even made strides into the Christian music industry. And this excellence didn't stop at the next generation. I remember conversations during my childhood about the colleges my cousins aspired to attend. It was never a question of *if* but *when* they would succeed.

I, on the other hand, grew up with learning disabilities. I was not good at reading or writing, and I was always terribly embarrassed about it. In fact, I spent most of my time trying to hide my struggle. I became super social to cover up my inability to perform academically and my subsequent humiliation. Heightening my sense of inferiority, I had an identical twin who was excellent in all the areas where I was subpar.

I would go to school and feel inadequate, and then I would go to church and feel the exact same way. I had been raised in the church, but I always felt pretty lost there. Actually, I felt a little lost in general. I did not have a natural, unique leadership gifting. I wasn't the person who was asked to do a lot in my community. I was the girl who flew under the radar, always overlooked and always dreaming, hoping I would one day be exceptional at something. I often thought that I just needed one big win—a triumph to confirm my value. Something that would make the struggle within me worth it. Maybe I thought success would make life easier and give me the inner confidence I so lacked. Little did I know that my internal battle—which I so hoped to throw off—would shape and influence my purpose and direction in life.

Backseat Breakthrough

We all have moments we want to forget. For me, it was my season in Yuba City. Don't get me wrong; it's a lovely, simple spot in Northern California, nestled between national forests and surrounded by farmlands. Yuba City was where my mom grew up, on a farm just outside of town. When my sister and I were fourteen, my parents made the decision to return, moving our family from Los Angeles to this small town so we could take care of my mom's ailing parents. In hindsight, the move also got us out of high school in LA and back to a simpler life.

I wasn't resistant to moving, but the pleasure and relief that might have come from suddenly slowing down and living a life that almost stood still was wasted on the teenage girl that I was. I felt lost. I was a sophomore in high school and, in my mind, we had left everything that seemed reasonable and comfortable behind in LA.

My learning issues didn't help, and I became obsessed with hiding them. Each year my lack of abilities became more apparent. My peers seemed to be running past me at warp speed, and I stood still. Paused in time. When someone would ask me what I was planning to do after high school, I would jokingly say, "My sister is preparing to go to nursing school, and I'm going to live off my parents." I was only halfway kidding because I didn't see success in my future. I was just surviving my daily battle.

So when we started over in a new place, I struggled even more to find my footing. I wasn't a popular girl at school. I held my own with advanced social skills, but my beauty didn't hold the room's attention, and I could easily slip through the halls unnoticed. For some reason, though, a group of guys made it their mission to get my sister's and my attention that year. Each weekend we would wake up to toilet paper in our front yard—that strange American tradition of creating a winter wonderland by throwing toilet paper as high as you can into someone's trees. The guys at school relentlessly pursued us, and it felt good to be noticed. Eventually we came around and began hanging out with them on the weekends—until one particular night.

I can't remember exactly when this happened. All I know is that it was dark in the car that evening, and I could feel the inside of my body moving to the beat of the music that was playing so loudly I could hardly think. Nothing could make me lose my mind like nineties R&B, and the gold 1973 Mustang convertible the guys had picked us up in wasn't helping. The windows were fogged up from the new rain, which had fallen a few minutes earlier, and the lack of airflow. I felt as if I belonged there, like the lyrics of the Tracy Chapman song "Fast Car": "I had a feeling that I belonged."

In some ways, it felt like any other night. We had been doing the exact same thing every weekend for months. If you had told me that this night would change my whole life, I wouldn't have believed you. But, in the darkness of that car, in the nauseating normal, something life changing happened.

My heart began to pound. In fact, the pounding was so hard my mind began to race, and the whole moment paused in time. I sensed something shifting in the car, which I can now say was the Holy Spirit. He immediately had my attention, and I began to hear him speaking to me in my heart.

He said, "Havilah, what are you doing? I've called you to more than living for the weekend. You cannot live like this anymore. You have a destiny and a calling. You've got to be courageous! Fight for your life! Get out of here!"

As my heart beat wildly, I felt I couldn't be silent any longer. I asked the guys to turn down the music so I could speak. Then I exclaimed, "I have a call of God on my life!"

I wish I could convey how awkward this moment was. There was no piano player or pastor in the background. No one nodding in affirmation as I made this life-changing proclamation. Quite the opposite. An uncomfortable silence filled the car, and the dark silhouettes of the two guys in the front seat didn't move. Nothing about it felt spiritual.

At this point, I burst into tears, overcome with the emotions I was feeling. As tears streamed down my face, I glanced at my sister. I wondered if she was going to act as if I were a crazy person who had lost her mind. But as I looked over at her, she was crying too. Something was happening in this car. She was experiencing the same thing I was.

In the middle of this awkward and holy moment, I blurted out to the guys, "You are welcome to come with me if you like, but even if you don't, this is what I'm going to do.

I'm going to follow God's calling." My final words were met with utter silence. No one said a thing, and as I continued to cry in the backseat, I felt an overwhelming peace and resolve settling inside of me.

Something had dramatically changed. Before, the approval of others had mattered to me deeply—but now, for the first time, I was free from that. I wasn't thinking about the guys. In fact, I didn't care anymore. No more hiding in the backseat of the car. No more feeling invisible in a very visible family. No more feeling left behind in my spiritual community.

Only one opinion mattered at that moment: God's! Even though I was not sure what the Holy Spirit's prompting would require going forward, I knew I had just made one of the most important decisions in my life: a wholehearted surrender to follow Jesus.

The Great Divide

Oswald Chambers called this point of decision in our lives the "Great Divide": "To get there is a question of will, not of debate nor of reasoning, but a surrender of will, an absolute and irrevocable surrender on that point."[1]

My "Great Divide" moment, my place of no return and complete surrender, happened in the backseat of a car. The guys didn't say anything after my proclamation, and I still laugh about it today. They took us home without saying a word. Later that night, as my sister and I knelt by our beds, I said this simple prayer out loud: "Lord, I am not much. I am young. I am a girl. I have absolutely no special gifts or graces in my life, but if you can use anyone, you can use me."

In that moment, I so wished the heavens would open and angels would appear. I wished for something supernatural to solidify the moment. But it didn't happen. Couldn't God have spared one angel? Just one? No. Not because he is mean or selective, but because he was trying to teach me a powerful lesson that I would remember to this day.

Simply put, he wanted me to understand that everything counts. No matter what we feel, what is happening around us, or how grand or quiet the moment is, the Lord hears what we say to him every single time. When you are praying and it seems as though you're not being heard, God is listening and taking you seriously. He hears that cry in your voice, in the deepest longing of your heart.

Perhaps we expect that once we've made the decision to surrender our lives to God, the heavens will open and things will automatically become easier—but that's not the case. In fact, some things get harder, and we struggle to see God in the middle of it all. Yet, as his children, we can be sure that on the battlefield of life, regardless of our current circumstances, he hears us. Faith is what matters to God, and if we reach out in faith, he will respond.

It's Not What You Think

The battles you face in life are not what you think they are. The battles involve more than you and your life. In fact, the war began long before your feet ever touched the soil of this planet.

Let's take a moment to go back to the beginning of the story.

Our enemy, the Devil, once lived in heaven (Rev. 12:9; 20:2). He was a created being. The Bible says he was an angel, and his body contained musical instruments (Ezek. 28:13). He was beautiful and more glorious than all the other angels, but pride, jealousy, and self-exaltation contaminated his heart. He didn't want to be merely a reflection of God; he wanted to dethrone God. He wanted the other angels' worship all to himself. He wanted the glory.

But God does not share his glory—not because he is selfish, but because he is wise and all-knowing. He knows the weight of his glory will destroy anyone who covets it. No one but God is capable of carrying such a high honor.

Still, Satan rallied one-third of the angels to join him in his doomed rebellion, and a war broke out in heaven. In the end, Satan and the fallen angels, now called demons, were cast out of heaven as punishment.

But the struggle continues on earth. This is where we come in.

Humans are God's most precious creation; we alone have been given the opportunity to become his sons and daughters. Satan knows this, and his revenge—his plan to get back at God—is to destroy our souls. As my friend Chris Durso once said, "Satan has already experienced heaven and knows he'll never be able to go back. So like a child, if he can't go, he doesn't want you to go."[2] The enemy is on a suicide mission. His destiny and eternal damnation are already set. His only goal now is to take as many people with him as he can. He wants people to worship him, which robs God of sons and daughters.

What does this look like in our everyday lives? Let's take a look at Eve and how Satan approached her all those years ago.

Most of us know the story of Adam and Eve, the first humans God created, and how he placed them in the paradise called the garden of Eden. There they lived peacefully and happily and walked closely with God. In fact, Genesis 3:8 tells us that God walked "in the garden in the cool of the day" (NKJV). What a joy it must have been to be in such close relationship with their maker! Then something happened to change everything. Enter Satan in the form of a serpent.

Genesis 3 tells us that the serpent approached Eve with a lie wrapped in truth. He posed a question about God, asking her if what he had heard was true:

> The serpent was clever, more clever than any wild animal GOD had made. He spoke to the Woman: "Do I understand that God told you not to eat from any tree in the garden?" (Gen. 3:1)

What a case of "fibs in a blanket"! Yes, God had told Adam and Eve earlier not to eat from one of the trees in the garden—but not all of them.

> GOD commanded the Man, "You can eat from any tree

in the garden, except from the Tree-of-Knowledge-of-Good-and-Evil. Don't eat from it. The moment you eat from that tree, you're dead." (Gen. 2:16–17)

Here we see the formation of a tactic the enemy commonly uses. The first thing he did, at the beginning of all beginnings, was to turn a statement into a question. We can assume the enemy wasn't confused, that he wasn't seeking clarity by asking that question. He was seeking engagement. Instead of clarity he wanted to bring confusion. He wanted Eve to become curious, because he knew her curiosity would lead to confusion—and confusion would result in the corruption of God's words to her.

Why was it so important to the enemy to distort God's words? He was trying to misrepresent God's intentions. He knew that if he could get Eve to grow curious, and eventually doubt God's intentions toward her, he could confuse her and contaminate what God had said. Distorting God's intentions was an entryway into Eve's heart—the entry point he needed.

I remember recognizing this strategy of the enemy years ago when I was having a heart-to-heart talk with God. I was sharing my sincere desire to live in a way that demonstrated my full trust in him. I asked him what a lifestyle of true trust looked like, and he said, "Havilah, true trust is believing my intentions toward you are always good."

I was speechless. I knew I didn't live with this reality.

Instantly, my eyes filled with tears, and my heart became heavy as I realized I didn't fully trust God. I had judged his intentions. I didn't believe him, or at least not as deeply as I could. He was asking me to return to the place my heart was created to live—a place of complete confidence.

Days and weeks after this realization, I would find myself in times of conflict and would hear him say to my heart, "Havilah, do you trust me? Do you believe my intentions toward you are only good?" Then I would feel the struggle inside. I resolved to listen to the Holy Spirit, knowing his voice would grow stronger in my heart if I focused on him. I was sure his love could overcome my greatest fear, so I would spend a moment releasing my fear and worry and leaning into trust, whispering under my breath, "Lord, I trust you. I believe you only have right motives toward me." In these moments of spiritual sobriety, peace would flood over my spirit and soul. I was gaining strength over the struggle.

One of my favorite verses that helps during the battle in our hearts over the truth of God's intentions goes like this: "'For I know the plans I have for you,' says the LORD" (Jer. 29:11 NLT). Another translation says, "I know what I'm doing. I have it all planned out—plans to take care of you, not abandon you, plans to give you the future you hope for."

The word *plans* in Hebrew is *machashabah*, which means "thoughts" and "purpose" but also "intentions." When I first learned this, it only confirmed the word God had given me the day of our heart-to-heart, and several other scriptures that do the same.

Psalm 40 says,

> Many, O LORD my God, are the wonderful works
> which You have done,

⌣

11

And Your thoughts toward us;

There is none to compare with You.

If I would declare and speak of your wonders,

They would be too many to count. (v. 5 AMP)

The word *thoughts* here is the same Hebrew word as the one translated as *plans* in Jeremiah. David was saying, "Your intentions toward us are wonderful and too many to count."

The enemy loves to prey on the places in our hearts where we don't trust God, where we don't believe his motive is good. He uses the parts of our stories where pain, abandonment, or rejection became our daily bread and then reminds us of those memories, of how we felt in those times, leading us to the conclusion that God is not who he says he is. Unlike God, Satan doesn't have our best interests in mind.

But the truth is, God would never tell us to do something without the best intentions. It's outside of his character to do or be anything but good.

Most of the time, when God tells us what to do, the enemy will ask questions that undermine what God has already clearly said. "God told you to do *what?*" the Devil asks. "Why would he do that? Is it that important?" His suggestions are meant to confuse us. The enemy will always try to change God's periods into question marks. He turns God's loving boundaries and instruction into a question of intention. I wonder how many of us start out taking God at his word but begin questioning him when the enemy comes inquiring.

God says, "You belong to me," and the enemy says, "Do you really belong to God?"

God says, "You are clean, washed white as snow," and the enemy says, "You're pure? Really?"

If we allow God's statements *to* us to change into questions *about* us, we will lack confidence. Our curiosity will lead to confusion, and eventually our enemy will corrupt what God said.

Jesus' half brother James warned us about this very thing, which he called being *double-minded*:

> If any of you lacks wisdom [to guide him through a decision or circumstance], he is to ask of [our benevolent] God, who gives to everyone generously and without rebuke or blame, and it will be given to him. But he must ask [for wisdom] in faith, without doubting [God's willingness to help], for the one who doubts is like a billowing surge of the sea that is blown about and tossed by the wind. For such a person ought not to think or expect that he will receive anything [at all] from the Lord, being a double-minded man, unstable and restless in all his ways [in everything he thinks, feels, or decides]. (James 1:5–8 AMP)

When we are double-minded, we stand "in the middle ground between faith and unbelief."[3] Until we come to a place in our lives where we firmly believe, "If God said it, then that settles it," we will never have peace, never be sufficiently stable in a turbulent world.

Your enemy's first attempt to cause instability and double-mindedness in your life will always cast doubt on what God asks you to do. The Devil's words will sound suspiciously like the truth but with a little spin added, including an evil intention.

The enemy used the same trick on Eve. He said, "Do I understand that God told you not to eat from any tree in the garden?" (Gen. 3:1). The Devil added the words *"any* tree," trying to question God's intention. Knowing his love for her, Eve should have been confident in God and his instructions, but she chose to have a conversation with the serpent when she should have walked away.

Most of us know the end of the story. Adam and Eve believed the lie that they could not fully trust God. They ate of the forbidden fruit, and the veil over their eyes was removed. They saw true evil and true good. Then they hid from God in shame, but he pursued them anyway. Leading them to confess, God came up with a plan to redeem them.

What was this most epic plan? Remember, the world was fallen, and man was now sinful; but God still wanted his creation to be able to spend eternity with him as sons and daughters. The problem was that evil and good could not reside in the same place, and humanity's sin deserved to be separated from God for all eternity—but God had a plan. He sent his only Son, Jesus, to die the death we deserved in order to set us free. Because of Christ's selfless act, we can now live with our Creator forever and ever.

I love how *The Message* translation explains it:

This is how much God loved the world: He gave his Son, his one and only Son. And this is why: so that no one need be destroyed; by believing in him, anyone can have a whole and lasting life. God didn't go to all the trouble of sending his Son merely to point an accusing finger, telling the world how bad it was. He came to help, to put the world right again. Anyone who trusts in him is acquitted; anyone who refuses to trust him has long since been under the death sentence without knowing it. And why? Because of that person's failure to believe in the one-of-a-kind Son of God when introduced to him. (John 3:16–18)

The day Jesus died on the cross, the battle was won. We don't have to find our own way to God. Jesus is the way, and if we fully trust in him, if we reach out to him in faith, he will respond. We will not be doomed to eternal damnation but instead will receive everlasting life. He is our way out! He is our truth and our life, the One we are looking for, the Savior.

How do we know this gift is ours?

Because if you acknowledge and confess with your mouth that Jesus is Lord [recognizing His power, authority, and majesty as God], and believe in your heart that God raised Him from the dead, you will be saved. (Rom. 10:9 AMP)

God only asks that we do two things to receive this gift of life. First, we acknowledge he is Lord. He deserves all glory, praise, and adoration. Second, we confess this acknowledgment with our mouths and submit to his leadership, living our lives fully for him.

Salvation is the good news. Rather, it's the *best* news we could ever receive! People of every generation, race, religion, gender, and background, those who are well educated or those who are uneducated, the everyday sinner or the greatest blasphemer—all can receive God's free and eternal gift if we will surrender to Jesus and reach out in faith. What a beautiful, triumphant victory in the war that started so long ago!

Why Am I Still Battling?

It's truly an amazing thing to be confident that our eternal life is set and that Jesus has already won the war, but oftentimes we notice we are still struggling. We ask questions such as, "If I'm following Christ, why do I still do things I don't want to do?" or, "Is it normal to battle while living faithfully?" We wonder, "Where is this battle coming from?"

Let me be the first to tell you that you are not alone in this. We all do battle each and every day. The war may have been won, but the battles are still a daily reality. The good news is, we have strategies to employ. But, first, let's take a look at some examples of everyday battles.

Internal

Our battles often come from inside once we accept our new identities in Christ.

Therefore if anyone is in Christ [that is, grafted in, joined to Him by faith in Him as Savior], he is a new creature [reborn and renewed by the Holy Spirit]; the old things [the previous moral and spiritual condition] have passed away. Behold, new things have come [because spiritual awakening brings a new life]. (2 Cor. 5:17 AMP)

I love how this verse reads: "He is a new creature [reborn and renewed by the Holy Spirit]." As soon as we receive Jesus, we become completely new people. If invited, the Holy Spirit will live inside of us and affirm what God is saying to us through his Word.

But even with the Holy Spirit, the Christian life is not always smooth sailing. Have you ever felt as if it isn't quite working for you the way it is supposed to? Have you ever thought someone else got more God than you did? I know I have—but why? It's because our minds, thoughts, attitudes, and beliefs must also be renewed. Yes! Our spirits want to agree with God, but our old lifestyles and habits of sin can trick us into believing we are not yet free. They lie to us. Our quickest and most powerful weapon, then, is to agree with truth. We need to ask ourselves, *What does God say about me?* If you know what he says, then you'll know how to do battle with what's coming out of the old you.

External

Sometimes the fight happens simply because we live in a fallen world.

Matthew 5:45 (NLT) says, "Your Father in heaven . . .

sends rain on the just and the unjust alike," which means no one is untouchable. Each life is touched by pain, sickness, and death. Life happens. Evil persists. The Devil is real. The fact that we face hard things doesn't always mean we are guilty of a specific crime. Suffering only confirms that an active battle still separates us from God.

Furthermore, God doesn't remove our power to choose good or evil. Our choice is vital to God's supernatural eco-system, because without choice there is no such thing as real love. Everyone must have an authentic opportunity to choose him or to choose evil. And sometimes this means other people will choose evil.

We have no power over other people's choices. Many of our battles are the results of people's wrong decisions, as they give themselves over to Satan's darkness. Their deci-sions have consequences that affect us no matter how much we are relying on God's guidance.

Theological

I once had a leader in my life who was excellent at mak-ing decisions. She seemed to have the secret sauce. Her choices were always embraced by the team in the end, even if they sometimes meant difficulty in the short-term.

One day I cornered her and asked, "When it comes to making a decision for your staff, what filter do you use?"

Without hesitation, she said, "I look for what's best for the rest."

I looked confused.

She explained, "When I make decisions, I look at what

will serve the greater whole rather than what will serve an individual or even myself. I don't mind making a choice that might cost someone something if it serves the greater whole."

God operates in the same way. Many of our personal battles feel deliberately put to us, and, well . . . let me explain.

God's mission is to gather as many souls on earth as are willing to live with him for eternity. He is passionate—no, vigilant—for everyone to have an opportunity to choose him. When we give our lives to him, his mission becomes our mission, though we don't see the whole picture as he does. We get caught up in our nearsighted natural and cultural realities.

So when we ask God to do something for us, our asking isn't wrong; in fact, he wants us to ask. But often he will answer with a "no" or "not yet." If we don't agree with his answer or don't want to wait, we struggle. We battle with his no. Sometimes we wonder if the Devil is withholding what we want from us. Sometimes we wonder if we lack the faith to move the hand of God. But in these cases, God is actually saying, "I'm going to do what's best for the rest. I have a plan. Trust me."

Each type of battle—internal, external, or theological—can leave us asking questions and struggling with life. Our questions may sound like this:

- Why am I on this earth?
- Is feeling lost normal?
- What is God's will for my life?
- Am I ever going to feel as though I have enough?

Maybe our questions go even deeper:

- Do I belong?
- Do I have what it takes?
- Am I replaceable?
- Can I really be happy?

Can I tell you something amazing? We don't need to feel continually caught in these questions and the struggles of life. I want to help blow the lid off of the enemy's plan and show you what he's been up to. I want to empower you to tread him underfoot and keep him there, right where he belongs.

Gone will be the days of constant warring, wondering if you have what it takes to belong to God. By walking this path together, we'll learn how to clearly know when the battle is coming from inside of ourselves, when the Devil is involved, and when God is intervening to give us a plan for battle.

We'll get practical and realistic. I'll tell you what's worked for me and share the small but radical shifts that have made a tremendous impact on my spiritual life. You can't win a battle if you don't have a fight plan—and God is ready to give you one.

This whole book is designed to crack open God's plan for your life. It will show you what a healthy spiritual life looks like and bring God's plan to the forefront. You'll begin to win in your everyday life.

So, my friend, let's jump in together and expose the truth.

EMPOWERMENT POINTS

- Everything counts. No matter what we feel, what is happening around us, or how grand or quiet the moment is, the Lord hears what we say to him every single time.
- God would never tell us to do something without the best intentions. It's outside of his character to do or be anything but good.
- If we allow God's statements to us to change into questions about us, we will lack confidence.
- Our battles often come from inside once we accept our new identities in Christ.
- The fight happens simply because we live in a fallen world.

Chapter 2

Two Camps

I generally have a hard time remembering exact situations and details about where I was or what I was doing on a day-to-day basis, but I have one memory that is as vivid and clear as if it happened last night.

I was just a teenager at the time and had joined a group of seventy-five others on a two-month mission trip traveling through seven states. Our purpose was to promote reconciliation with tribal communities, and we were spending our summer washing the feet of Native Americans and smoking the peace pipe of God's love. Hoping to bring to light God's heart for the reservations, our group sang and danced every evening for small groups across the Midwest. After our first month out, we finally started to hit our stride.

On this particular night, we finished our performance and

then huddled together in the back of the church to pray. Some kneeled, and others stood. We worshiped with a simple guitar and our voices. Suddenly, a startling cry rang out in the room. Deciphering the noise was initially hard, but as we listened, it became clearer. It wasn't a cry of sorrow or a sob of adoration. Instead, it was very distinct and direct. We all stood there, paralyzed, as we watched a young girl on the other side of the room begin to scream, shake, and convulse. Having never seen anything like that before, I was terrified. No one dared to move.

Time seemed to stand still as we watched the horror unfolding before our eyes. Finally, a leader rushed over to the girl and began giving directions: "I want everyone to grab hands with each other. Form a circle!"

We immediately began to shuffle. I don't know if we had a clear sense of order or if we were just so shocked that we grabbed one another's hands out of fear.

The leader stepped into the middle of the circle with the girl in her arms and said in a firm voice, "I want you to turn this circle inside out. Don't face her, but turn your backs, link arms, and pray."

A soft thunder of voices filled the place as we each prayed fervently.

An hour passed, and the strange noises continued. Commanding voices rose up behind our backs, but no one turned around. I think we all remembered God commanding Lot and his family not to turn around and watch the destruction of Sodom and Gomorrah in the Bible. No one wanted to end up as a salt lick for the Devil.

As the room finally quieted, the girl was whisked away to

another room, and our trip leaders gently encouraged us to head off to bed and get some sleep. Sleep? I think not. That night we all lay in the darkness, eyes wide open, still scared out of our minds. No one made a peep.

We all had many questions running around in our heads, so much we didn't know, but none of us felt brave enough to talk about it. We all should have known what was going on, but we weren't brave enough to ask for a conversation about what we had just experienced. Instead, our leader came in the next morning and carried on as though nothing had happened. Feeling as if, somehow, we'd all been sworn to secrecy, no one ever talked about that night again. At least not with our spiritual leaders.

Now, more than twenty years later, as I reflect on that eventful night, I can't help but feel a little frustrated. Why didn't someone tell us what was going on? Didn't our leaders realize we would have questions and fears after such an emotional event?

The truth was, they did answer—just not with words. The implied answers were clear: "You are not ready for what's in that circle. Only certain people are prepared and anointed to deal with the supernatural. Maybe one day you will have this grace and power, but for now, it's scary and vague, dangerous and powerful, hidden and possibly contagious."

Many of us have faced spiritual experiences that leave us feeling more like outsiders than insiders. These experiences cause us to ask questions like, "If I'm supposed to live in the light, how come I've been left in the dark?"

You may feel as spiritually unprepared as I did—not

understanding what's actually happening. Maybe you feel as if the enemy is too powerful to try to fight. In these moments, we can be made to feel as though we aren't important enough to know everything, like the kid sent out of the room so Mom and Dad can talk.

As I've thought about that night over the years, my amazement and frustration took me to the Word. I wanted to figure out what all the secrecy was about, to know everything I could about this often-forbidden topic. I wanted to find out if there were any supernatural deal breakers when it came to the enemy and his schemes. I wanted to be crystal clear about his place, his power, and his presence in our lives.

And today, I'm inviting you into that inner circle of understanding. I want us to personally and corporately turn back around, grab hands, and look at what's going on. I want us to find ourselves motivated to learn what the Bible has to say. Furthermore, I want us to be profoundly empowered. When someone asks you about the Devil, his schemes, or how to live with him on this same round earth, I want you to be able to smile because you're exceptionally qualified to answer. Kick fear to the curb and become fully awake, knowing exactly how to deal with your enemy. Let us live the lives God intended us to live all along.

Defensive Modes

Before we can be empowered to deal with the supernatural, we must understand our natural responses when confronted with our enemy. To identify and explain what many of us deal with on a regular basis, I have taken the liberty to outline some of our natural defense modes. These unprocessed inclinations can leave us feeling emotionally, mentally, and even spiritually defensive.

When our minds pick up any sign of potential danger, they instantly react to defend us by launching a *fight, flight,* or *freeze* response. New York University neuroscientist Joseph LeDoux calls these responses "survival circuits"[1] that we all have, buried deep in the automatic system of our brains. For example, imagine yourself crossing the road. Everything is clear until a car comes out of nowhere and almost hits you. You don't have time to think about how you will act. Your automatic reactions take over. First, you freeze, paralyzed by sudden fear. Once your brain computes what's happening, you jump out of the way. It happens so quickly that you barely have time to think. As your thoughts become clearer, you yell at the driver as he drives away. The event is over in seconds.

Our brains function in a particular way when they sense danger. The part of you that stopped you in your tracks is the automatic *freezing* posture. The sudden force to jump back and get out of the way comes from your automated *flight.* When you yelled at the car, the *fight* in your brain was engaged. All of these responses are hardwired—but they're not always the most helpful. Let's take a closer look together.

Freeze

Freezing is the simplest of the three defensive modes and is often a posture we take naturally just before we move on to either fight or flight. How often have you stopped right in your tracks when you felt powerless? I've been guilty of freezing right in the middle of a critical moment. I just short-circuit. The instinct is grounded in fear as I try to assess the problem and then rapidly locate the appropriate solution.

Freezing is a normal reaction. We freeze when we feel an overwhelming sense of confusion or anxiety, unsure of what path to take. It reminds me of the phrase "paralyzed with fear." We'll talk more about having a plan for fear later on in the book, so if you feel stuck or powerless right now, hang on. Standing in a defensive posture doesn't have to last forever.

Flight

I was raised on the road. My dad was an ordained minister who traveled eight months out of the year. Our little family would go with him for six of these months. We spent our time in churches all over the world, conservative and charismatic, missional and seeker-sensitive, denominational and nondenominational. I grew up experiencing the church at large.

As if that wasn't enough, I started to travel and minister at the age of eighteen. I've spent almost my whole life in faith communities. It doesn't take long to realize the pretty clear differences between our various faith communities. Even though we all read the same Bible, different things stand out in each subgroup of the body of Christ. For lack of a better term, we'll call them *camps*.

One camp never talks about the enemy. When something strange happens in the supernatural realm, they deal with it as quickly and as quietly as possible. Moreover, there is usually a particular person in their community assigned to deal with anything that looks strange or supernatural—so those who are not assigned to this task are unfamiliar with the supernatural. A common reaction to the unfamiliar, especially the unfamiliar supernatural, is to run. This instinct is hardwired within our neurological makeup.

It's easy to see why part of the church goes into flight mode when it comes to supernatural battles. They may repeat scriptures such as, "The enemy is under our feet," but in reality, they don't understand what it looks like to stand up and fight because they've never learned. For these camps, any sign of spiritual warfare elicits fear and worry. The idea of it feels out of control. Scary. Running seems like the safest way to respond.

Back in the day, a woman in our church had dark skin, a fire-red pantsuit, and a diamond pin clipped to her lapel that flashed the name of Jesus. If the blinding brooch didn't stop you in your tracks, the fire in her eyes proved she wasn't messing around. I remember watching supernatural activity flaring up among people in our community a few times, and the church leaders would quickly take action by taking them to another room. This fiery lady would follow close behind, and the crowd would let out a silent sigh of relief—almost as if to say, "If Sister So-and-So is taking care of it, then we are good to go!"

After some time away, the people who had exited would all come back into the main room. The fiery woman still wore a vibrant smile across her face, and inevitably the

individual who'd been experiencing the supernatural occur-
rence would rejoin us with a look of relief and a face puffy
from crying. Slowly the room would return to normal. That
was just how we handled those events. No questions asked.

When you grow up in a spiritual home like this, the
lesson you learn is: "Spiritual warfare is a scary thing. God
gives specific people grace to deal with demons and the
spiritual world, but you are probably not one of them. You
should leave it alone." And so the natural response when
something *does* happen is to flee.

Fight

Another side of the church community reacts in the
exact opposite way. It seems to be especially interested in
fighting the enemy. This camp exhibits a "Here a devil,
there a devil, everywhere a devil, devil" mentality. Most of
its sermons, songs, and prayers focus on the enemy, and its
people live with an aggressive, high-alert warfare outlook.

If their cars run out of gas, they say, "The Devil made
it happen." If they find themselves in a fight with their
spouses, they say, "The Devil is attacking us." Anything and
everything can be blamed on the Devil, and their struggles
are always connected to the enemy. Every trial. Each sickness. All heartache.

Most of these spiritual communities use scriptures such
as, "The devil prowls around like a roaring lion looking for
someone to devour" as their warfare education (1 Peter
5:8 NIV). They seem to live with a sense of seriousness and
urgency when it comes to all spiritual matters. They think,

God might be winning, but only because we are fighting along-side him. Our struggle is the deciding factor. Our attention must be on him at all times.

The lesson that most have learned growing up in a spiritual home like this is: "Spiritual warfare is a way of life. The battle is being waged, and I'm in the middle of it. If I don't stay alert and aware, I might lose the power and authority over my life to the enemy." So, in this situation, the natural response is to fight.

Defense Versus Discovery

I came across an interesting concept about the brain the other day while I was reading Caroline Webb's book *How to Have a Good Day*. In it, she explains that each of our brains has two modes of response to the outside world: a defensive system and a reward system.[2]

We investigated our normal reactions to threat earlier when we discussed our defense modes. These responses often don't give us the most positive outcomes when we lean too far into them, but there is another path we should consider. While threats put us in defense mode, finding delight or potential rewards and opportunities in our situations puts us in discovery mode. In defense mode, our focus is to protect ourselves. In discovery mode, our focus is to open up and learn. Discovery mode is simply a healthy way of staying curious. It allows our minds to stay open to new possibilities, concepts, and belief systems.[3]

Reacting in a defense mode isn't wrong. God created us that way—for our preservation! We are supposed to perceive threats as potentially damaging and, therefore, respond to them. But if we are always defensive—seeing all circumstances as threats and not opportunities for growth, never moving from a self-protecting and self-preserving shoreline to an inquisitive, Spirit-filled, deep-water swim—we will lose our appetite for the supernatural. We will only understand the supernatural as a means to an end, not as a life-giving partnership with the Holy Spirit at work in our everyday lives.

When the church exists in defense mode, our predictable reaction is to have a heightened sense of awareness. We either run away from it, pretending that the threat we feel is not real or not our business, or we find ourselves looking around every corner in anticipation of a sudden hostile takeover. Whether we are running, hiding, and ignoring, or, on the other side of the coin, focusing, glorifying, and obsessing, we are in defense mode.

Why is it vital that we move from defense mode to discovery mode when it comes to spiritual warfare?

Always being in defense mode doesn't just hinder us; it stops us. We become limited when making important life choices because we only perceive the threat. We feel weighed down by being on the alert at all times. Living with a heightened state of awareness drains us and eventually wears us out. We weren't made to be one fight away from defeat all the time.

If we can move from defense mode to discovery mode,

our ability to see the reward will explicitly empower our daily lives. We will go from feeling as if we're always battling to having a general sense of winning. We might be able to live in the defense, but we can thrive in the state of discovery, knowing we are called to a place of victory.

I'm confident that if you're holding this book, you are ready for this different approach.

Let's look at a few things together that can help us move to discovery mode.

James 4:7 says, "So submit to [the authority of] God. Resist the devil [stand firm against him] and he will flee from you" (AMP). Rick Renner unpacks this scripture for us:

> The word "resist" is from the Greek word *anthistemi*, which is a compound of the words *anti* and *istimi*. The word *anti* means *against, as to oppose something.* The word *istimi* means *to stand.* When placed into one word, thus forming the word *anthistemi*, it means *to stand against* or *to stand in opposition.* It is a word that demonstrates *the attitude of one who is fiercely opposed to something and therefore determines that he will do everything within his power to resist it, to stand against it, and to defy its operation.*[4]

This command to resist doesn't portray a passive church. It paints the picture of a church ready to fiercely oppose the enemy and do everything in her power to stand against him. You may be wondering what the difference is between standing in defense mode and resisting in discovery mode. It all comes down to the belief behind the action. When we stand in a defensive position, we do so out of fear. When we stand in a resisting position, we do so out of power and anointing and a surety of our victory. We have all the authority we need to command the enemy to leave, and when we do, he must go. No questions asked.

When we are learning something new that's foreign to our spiritual senses, it's common to revert to defense mode. We must resist this tendency. If we can defy the urge to fight, take flight, or freeze, we can acclimate to a spiritual place of discovery—a place where we understand that defensiveness limits our spiritual awareness but discovery helps us realize our spiritual power. We quickly move from protecting ourselves to focusing on the bigger picture of Jesus' victory and the reward that victory gives us, which is the authority to resist the Devil.

The Authority of the Hero

Perhaps, like me, you have felt powerless despite what Scripture says. Maybe you have felt left in the dark or like a spiritual outsider, or just not spiritual enough. Each experience can leave you fixated on what you're *not* rather than on who God says you *are*.

A few years back, I was ministering in a church. During the service, some people gathered around a woman in the front and prayed for her. Suddenly she collapsed and began to shake. It was hard to see exactly what was taking place because a group of people surrounded her. They quickly ran up to me, asking if I would come and pray over her. I asked them if the pastor was there, to which they replied, "Yes, in fact, several are around her."

I looked at them and said, "No, I think you guys have it covered."

Why would I respond this way?

Perhaps this will help.

Donald Miller explains the power of story in his StoryBrand course. The Insta-story goes like this: Donald went away to a cabin to write a book but found himself up in the woods, unmotivated and uninspired. He didn't have Wi-Fi but had a case of old DVDs. As he procrastinated, he decided to watch the most popular and familiar titles, including *Tommy Boy*, *Star Wars*, *Bridget Jones's Diary*, *The Hunger Games*, *Moneyball*, and *The King's Speech*. As he watched the different films, he began to see a pattern. Grabbing a notepad and a pen, he took notes. Eventually the seven elements to a great story emerged.

Amid the story elements, Donald discovered a powerful way to develop stronger marketing messages by structuring them into a seven-part framework. You'd have to take his StoryBrand course to learn all seven, but one interesting part that stood out to me was the role of the hero. Donald explained that people want to be the heroes in their own stories, not secondary characters who watch someone else be the hero. He related it to the Star Wars series and explained that people aren't looking for someone else to be Luke Skywalker in their stories; they want other people to be Yoda. If you're not familiar with Star Wars, I'll just say

Yoda's purpose in the series is to be a guide. His primary role is to teach Luke how to be the hero.

When I watched this course and first heard this revelation, I sat back in my chair. I was feeling emotional, which seemed like a strange reaction. I began to ask myself some questions. In a moment several life experiences flashed through my mind. I saw for the first time that most of my previous church experiences having to do with supernatural occurrences had been tied to the pastor or leader being the hero. As young people, we would listen to stories that placed our leaders at the center of the narrative rather than as guides. I don't think any of us in the church ever saw our leaders as Yoda, but instead as Luke Skywalker. The church story didn't put the believer in the middle; the church put its leaders in the middle. Why was this?

Leaders are human, and some leaders are very insecure. Their strength comes from being the most spiritual-looking person in the room. So when supernatural happenings arise, whether they're aware of this or not, they love keeping others in the dark because it makes them feel powerful. I often see those who teach on the supernatural be aloof, eccentric, and independent. They may be well intentioned, but when they are quick to be the hero, people start abandoning the community. Churchgoers grow tired of sitting in the background and paying homage by orbiting around their leader. Inevitably, they realize their beloved leader has no intention of making them heroes in their own stories but is happily being the hero for everyone. So people leave, saying, "I just don't think I fit here anymore," or, "I need something different." Leaders may feel betrayed, but it's a natural outcome when a church puts all its focus on a few central people. Instead of falling into this trap, we must go back to the example of Jesus. He didn't demand to be lifted high at the expense of others in order to feel spiritual or powerful. In fact, he often called out religious leaders for doing this very thing.

But our leaders aren't the only ones to blame. We've been placing leaders in the hero role for thousands of years. When the Israelites, God's people, were given a choice between having God or a king, they quickly picked a king. They wanted someone else to talk to God for them. A buffer. A scapegoat. We are guilty of the same tendency. We are quick to idolize—placing leaders in Christian celebrity positions and asking them what they think before asking God in prayer.

Let's be honest. Being the hero is not easy, and sometimes it feels safer letting our leaders be the heroes of our stories. Stepping into our true identities and taking on spiritual battles comes at a real cost. Along with fully living and taking ownership of the authority God offers us comes the possibility of disappointment, rejection, and sometimes failure. But it's how we were created to live. Yes, there are tough realities we will have to face, but an irreplaceable sense of fulfillment and contentment accompanies stepping into our daily spiritual battles with purpose and confidence. Nothing can replace living in the sweet spot of life, going after God-sized dreams, and getting into the ring to fight the good fight of faith. What an amazing adventure—and we each have a leading role.

So, let's go back to the moment when the people at the church asked me if I would come pray over the woman who had suddenly collapsed and started shaking. Why did I respond the way I did?

Every one of those people had the authority to deal with what was happening. They didn't need some traveling minister to come over and be the hero in the story. Each one of them was a hero in the story, anointed to deal with the Devil. If they didn't have anyone else to pray for the woman in need, then by all means, I would have gone. But they had it covered. They just needed to be reminded.

I want to remind you that you are the hero in your story too. As a Christian, you are anointed to deal with the Devil and win every time. This promise was spoken to you in the book of Isaiah:

> "No weapon that is formed against you will succeed;
>   And every tongue that rises against you in judgment you will condemn.
>   This [peace, righteousness, security, and triumph over opposition] is the heritage of the servants of the LORD,
>   And this is their vindication from Me," says the LORD. (54:17 AMP)

Did you catch that? *"No weapon that is formed against you."* Not only do you hold the advantage; you *are* the advantage.

The Message version of the Bible says,

> "But no weapon that can hurt you has ever been forged.

Any accuser who takes you to court will be dismissed as a liar.

This is what GOD's servants can expect.

I'll see to it that everything works out for the best."

GOD's Decree.

"This is what God's servants can expect." Come on! We can know for certain, each and every day, that we live on a fallen earth with our real enemy but can still expect everyday wins.

Several years ago, my husband and I purchased a new home. We were excited to move into our new Casa Cunnington, but our excitement quickly faded. Each night we would go to bed and have a horrible night's sleep. We were all having bad dreams; our sleep was restless and interrupted. At first I didn't notice anything especially concerning, but after a continual disturbance, I called a friend who was an intercessor and had a gift of understanding the spirit realm. I told her what had been happening and asked her what I should do. She suggested taking a night as a family to pray over the property, anointing the four corners of our land and declaring it holy. She explained that any spiritual atmosphere that was still lingering needed to be reminded of the authority we have in Christ.

So we did just that. We gathered our young family and marched to each corner of our land with a jar of oil. We prayed. We declared that we had authority and that any tormenting spirit had to exit the premises. We symbolically anointed the doorposts with oil and thanked God for our beautiful home. We didn't go crazy with chanting, crying, or dancing. Nope. We just held a simple time of prayer and worship.

At the time we didn't feel anything spectacular, but we were confident in our authority. After that night, we had the best night's sleep we'd had in weeks. Whatever had been lingering was removed. We submitted to God and resisted the enemy—and he left. Done and done!

One of the most important things to remember as we face our everyday battles is that standing and resisting doesn't mean being weird. We don't have to act spiritually creepy. God isn't asking us to stir up all kinds of crazy forces or to go after realms we have no business going after. If you run into spiritual resistance in some area of your life, simply take authority and move on. The enemy loves chaos, fear-driven prayers, and an overspiritualized atmosphere, because he loves for us to waste our time focusing on him. Don't give in to that.

No matter your experiences or the teachings you've heard about spiritual warfare, whether your church has been afraid of spiritual things or has bordered on obsession and glorification, we need re-education on spiritual warfare. Gross misconceptions and elitism have kept most of the church in the dark about their power to win daily battles with the enemy.

Enough of the fear-based messages. Enough of our obsession with darkness. Let's get back to what Jesus wanted us to know from the beginning. No shortcuts, no secret handshakes, no misleading spirituality. Let's get back to the uncomplicated gospel, the straightforward certainty Christ came to bring. Let's get back to claiming our spiritual authority, believing that the same spirit that raised Christ from the dead is now living in us.

Let's get back to winning every day.

EMPOWERMENT POINTS

- Many of us have faced spiritual experiences that leave us feeling more like outsiders than insiders.
- A common reaction to the unfamiliar, especially the unfamiliar supernatural, is to run.
- When the church exists in defense mode, our predictable reaction is to have a heightened sense of awareness.
- Living with a heightened state of awareness drains us and eventually wears us out.
- You are anointed to deal with the Devil and win every time.

Chapter 3

A Fight Worth Fighting

My mom was a softball champion. Her claim to fame was winning the local softball championship as her team's catcher. She loved the game. As early as I can remember, she was signing up my sister and me to play ball. We were thrilled, and everyone got to play! The experience was all about enjoying the game and learning to play.

But eventually, the older I got, the more the game became about winning. Those who played well were on the field, and those who didn't . . . well, we sat on the bench. My sister and I were affectionately called benchwarmers. We tried, but we just didn't play well. My mom would come to every game to cheer us on enthusiastically. Week after week, game after game, we sat. I remember asking her one day in high school, "Mom, can you come at the end of the game?"

She looked puzzled.

"It's just that . . . well, I don't play until the end." Usually, if we were winning, I got to play at the end because my performance couldn't hurt the outcome. Or, if we were losing, the coach would put me in because—you guessed it—it still couldn't hurt. Having my mother come and sit through the whole game, only to possibly see me play one inning, was humiliating.

I think we all can relate to a moment in life when we didn't end up winning. Maybe you suffered this kind of embarrassment in school like I did, or maybe you felt it amid social settings growing up. Some of us lost because of our parents, who never built healthy relationships with us. Many of us lost moments in our lives to trauma and abuse. Our innocence was robbed from us, and we are still trying to regain parts of our stories. You may have lost time in childhood due to sickness, or maybe illness has kept you from enjoying the life you longed to live. Regardless of your specific circumstances, loss is a human condition we universally understand.

Considering this, are we all really supposed to win in life? I know the word *win* can send some of us spiraling. How can we talk about winning if we are barely getting by? We start thinking about all the wins we still need for our lives to seem successful, and we wonder if we ought to be competing against someone else or even ourselves.

Let me remind you of something. We didn't start out life disappointed. We didn't start out cynical. Every healthy child begins life wanting to enjoy and learn, to be loved and included. God created us that way. As a mother, I didn't have to teach my boys to want to play. They came out ready and willing—willing to win at life. They looked at life unfiltered. If they saw it, then they believed they could do it. Success was that simple for them.

You were created the same way. You came into life willing to try, wanting to participate and be included. You began with a profound sense of enjoyment and delight. You weren't swayed by others' opinions or their perspectives because you didn't even know they had them. You only knew your limitations by trial and error. You were willing to try.

For most of us, though, we quickly learned that life was more about winning than enjoying—which is frustrating, because winning is an ever-moving target. Our worldly expectations of success and victories often turn into experiences that look more like failures, limitations, and losses.

I'll never forget the time I ran to the altar with tears streaming down my face as a seventeen-year-old. I knelt near the front, wanting to make myself as invisible as I felt. Pouring out my heart to God, I began to explain to him my lack. I said, "God, my hands are so empty. I have nothing to offer you, nothing you can use that is evident to me."

I was ready for him to disqualify me, but he gently responded, "Yes, Havilah, your hands are empty now, but one day I will fill them to overflowing."

His words were like a light at the end of a tunnel. I couldn't see how he was going to do it, but I believed what he said. I would just have to trust him and keep going forward.

Now, all these years later, I see how he kept his promise to me. What I couldn't see then—which he had in full view—was my potential.

God will always see past our lack, past our pain, and speak to the person we are becoming. He is calling us to develop our spiritual lives. You may have lost in the world, but you're not a loser to God. You may have failed, but you're not a failure. God doesn't talk down to you. He isn't grading you. You are not disqualified. He will always speak to you from the viewpoint of your potential, from the highest place.

If you had asked me years ago what God was like, I might have answered, "God is love," but I honestly wouldn't have given it much thought. I figured he was kind of an upset God. I imagined him busily monitoring everyone's lives, frustrated by their choices. If he wasn't angry, I was sure he was grieved, sitting in a dazed state, looking at the world in shock, ignoring us until we did the things that got his attention. I bet many people have this conception of God. We are often so busy wondering what God wants or needs from us, but we don't spend nearly as much time contemplating his feelings and thoughts toward us.

It wasn't until I heard a message on the subject of God liking us that my idea of God changed. Mike Bickle's message changed my entire theology that day, and thus my whole life.

He taught about the words David wrote in Psalm 149:

> For the LORD takes pleasure in His people;
> He will beautify the humble with salvation. (v. 4 AMP)

The thought that God not only liked me, but that he enjoyed me, took me off guard. God wasn't angry, sad, or distant. He was a happy God. He didn't just love me, but he liked me . . . delighted in me. This changed everything.

Once I let this reality soak into my spirit, I began to see his leadership in a whole new light. Before, I'd often imagined God standing right next to me, seeing my life from my perspective. But now I imagine God sees so much more. Yes, he will never leave our sides, but he exists outside of our moment-to-moment conception of time. He stands at the place where we could end up if we follow his direction. He's looking at us and saying, "Surrender that to me. You aren't going to need it," or, "Build right where you are!" He might even be telling us to make significant changes in our lives.

To someone without God's vision, his direction may seem confusing or look like a step back, but only God knows where we need to go. He is omniscient and present everywhere at the same time. Only his leadership is perfect for our lives. Yes, he is right beside us, comforting us, but he is also at the finish line encouraging and affirming our steps of faith. He is pulling us forward with his words.

I realize no one may have taught you this before, but I'm going to give it to you straight. You weren't meant just to live. You weren't intended just to get by. God didn't create anyone to live for the weekends. He didn't die on a cross so we could snuggle up to shame, fear, or failure. He died to give us full access to everything he has to give, which is more than we could imagine.

"That is what the Scriptures mean when they say, 'No eye has seen, no ear has heard, and no mind has imagined what God has prepared for those who love him'" (1 Cor. 2:9 NLT).

The truth is, you can't live a fulfilled and winning life if you don't take your life seriously. Living a spiritually authentic life is your responsibility alone. No one can preach, pray, or talk enough to get you out of apathy. Some of us are struggling—that's normal—but the rest of us may be catering to spiritual laziness.

At the end of the day, the answer isn't "being true to yourself," as the world might say; the answer is being true to God. Left to yourself, you will only bring destruction to your life. You'll go bankrupt mentally, emotionally, and spiritually. Only God knows how to love you. But you have to follow him to get all of him. It's that simple.

Running to Win

How do we contain and sustain the life we've been promised? Answer: only by having an authentic and active relationship with the Holy Spirit. It's impossible for us to be alive on the inside without the help of the Spirit.

In chapter one, I briefly explained why we struggle, even though we have the Spirit of God living inside of us. Let's take a deeper look at this truth.

Awhile ago I was speaking at a conference, and my husband, Ben, came to support me. We landed late, so we only had time to run into our hotel room and throw our bags open. We needed to change, freshen up, and run out the door as quickly as possible. I was almost ready when I asked Ben to help me save time by grabbing a three-strand necklace out of my jewelry bag. He rushed into the bedroom as I spackled another layer of makeup onto my face. After a while there was no sight of Ben, so I called out to him, asking if everything was okay. He walked back into the bathroom with a handful of jewelry. Once I saw it, I knew I was in trouble. Every woman reading this book right now knows what I'm talking about.

No matter how much you organize your jewelry for a trip, it always ends up in a ball. I quickly grabbed the bunch and began to work on separating the strings. At one point, I thought I had finally untangled them all, only to find them still intertwined. I finally gave up and threw the whole ball away after spending a ridiculous amount of time working on it. Insert audible groan!

Hebrews 12 reads, "Therefore, since we are surrounded by such a great cloud of witnesses, let us throw off everything that hinders and the sin that so easily entangles. And let us run with perseverance the race marked out for us, fixing our eyes on Jesus, the pioneer and perfecter of faith" (vv. 1–2 NIV).

"*The sin that so easily entangles.*" The word *entangle* in Greek refers to something that clings so tightly that it impedes movement. Our sinful habits do just that. They choke the life out of us, clinging to us even as we prepare to run the race of our spiritual journey. We cannot hold on to these sins if our goal is to win. And Paul, the apostle of Jesus who wrote two-thirds of the New Testament, tells us in 1 Corinthians that this is exactly what our goal should be: "You've all been to the stadium and seen the athletes race. Everyone runs; one wins. Run to win. All good athletes train hard. They do it for a gold medal that tarnishes and fades. You're after one that's gold eternally" (9:24–25).

He reminds us that we're not just running to win a gold medal. We run for an eternal prize that can never be destroyed. But running sounds easy until you actually try to live victoriously. We struggle as our sins entangle us and hold us back. Just like my ball of jewelry, life can become a tangled mass and lose its value. We are so intertwined with old thoughts, a stubborn will, and controlling emotions that we feel like giving up and throwing away our hope for the future. If you have experienced this, take a deep sigh of relief. You're normal.

The epicenter of this battle is within our souls, because our souls—otherwise known as our "flesh" in the Bible—are continually in the process of being transformed. Our spirits may be awakened and made new after first accepting the lordship of Jesus, but our souls still have a journey ahead.

But, what's the difference between our souls and our spirits? The soul is where the mind, will, and emotions live. Our mind encompasses our thoughts, our emotions are where our feelings reside, and our will is where our determination and decisions originate. Our spirits, on the other hand, are the redeemed parts of who we are. When we allow Jesus to be our Savior and Lord, our spirits are instantaneously renewed, immediately filled with God's life. Prior to this, our spirits were dead like deflated balloons. The moment we invite God to come live in our hearts, the Holy Spirit comes inside and fills our spirits with his life.

The Holy Spirit is not a part of the package; he's the whole package. When we open our hearts to him, we get all of him. We were created with a God-shaped hole inside, and the Holy Spirit fills it perfectly. We become new creations. Our spirits start working correctly, and we receive everything God intended when he first created us. Second Corinthians puts it this way: "This means that anyone who belongs to Christ has become a new person. The old life is gone; a new life has begun!" (5:17 NLT).

Our lives should not be labeled as failing, lacking, humiliating, purposeless, or powerless in any way. Our lives should be overflowing with purpose and hope. We should be walking every day with a zest for life—with a constant vigor and gusto.

But what happens when our souls haven't quite caught up with our spirits? What happens when our minds, wills, and emotions get tangled up as we run the race? How do we contain and sustain this life we've been promised? We prevail by having an authentic and active relationship with the Holy Spirit. It's impossible to be alive on the inside without the Creator of life.

Defining Success

Some people already understand that we should win in life and appear to be experiencing a measure of success. At the same time, many Christ followers still struggle with feelings of failure, disappointment, and guilt. I will confess that I sometimes move back and forth between these two positions. It can be hard to stay grounded in the victory we long for so deeply. Many of us aren't sure where these defeatist feelings come from, and we live embarrassed and ashamed that we must fight to win every day.

Let's unpack this for a bit.

We need to ask ourselves a vital question: How should we define success in life? Let's consider the late John Wooden's words. He was a committed Christian who became the most successful college basketball coach in history. In the world's eyes, he would have personified complete success, but when asked how he defined success, he replied, "Success is peace of mind which is a direct result of self-satisfaction in knowing you did your best to become the best you are capable of becoming."[1] In other words, winning means living as you were created to live: with confidence in knowing you did your best.

I was getting ready one morning, listening to one of my favorite podcasts. On the show, a psychologist takes calls on the air and answers questions, and on this day, a mother called in about her husband's response to their grade-school children. She explained that her husband was very hard on their kids about their grades, and the mother wanted to know if it was reasonable for the father to expect so much. The doctor answered, "Specific expectations can be harmful and, in some cases, abusive." She then said something that turned a lightbulb on inside me: "It can be detrimental if you expect more from your child than their personal best."

Where do these kinds of harmful expectations come from? I believe we are fed a handful of lies early on, and we continue to swallow them now—especially in American culture.

The first lie many of us have believed is, "If you work hard enough, you can be anything you want to be." In other words, our desire can outweigh our gifts, graces, and education. If we want it bad enough, we will gain it. We just have to believe!

The second lie is, "You have to be the best in the world to be truly successful." People spend their whole lives believing the only marker of success is being at the top. You can't just do a good job, provide for your family, and give to those around you. You must be the most influential, powerful, educated, gifted, and stunning person in the room. Success looks like winning gold medals, being valedictorian, earning your master's degree, and coming in first place.

Why are these beliefs dangerous? Is it wrong to dream of success? The truth is, we can't always grow up to be anyone we want to be, no matter what we've been told.

I laughed when I saw this meme on Pinterest the other day: "As a young child, my mother told me I could grow up to be anything I want to be. It turns out this is called *identity theft*."

Hilarious, but accurate.

Also, if success is about needing to be at the top, you can't stay at the top forever. Eventually someone will replace you. If personal success is grounded in position, status, beauty, influence, or title, every victory will be momentary. But if our success is defined in a God-directed way, we will live fulfilling and successful lives knowing we became our personal best.

What does this have to do with our spiritual development? Let's look at this a little further.

I live with boys. Actually, I live in a house of only boys—five of the most incredible, wild, sometimes gross, but always active man cubs. We even recently got a male puppy to expand our boy tribe. Truth be told, the state of being surrounded by only men is completely new to me. I grew up in a home full of women. I had my mom, my twin sister, and an Italian dad who was almost a girl. I'm kidding, but he was the emotional one. He would cry more than us, talk more than us, and hold his own when it came to heart-to-heart talks. When I married Ben, it was the first time I lived with a typical man. If he had a feminine side to him, he sure hid it well. And that was okay with me. I'm fine being the only girl.

Having lived with my dad and now the five men in our home, I can say this with full confidence: No two men are the same or created equal. They are unique individuals.

If you were to ask me who is the most successful of all the men in my family, I would say my husband—because he married me. I'm kidding! No, I would say each of them is outstanding, because each is an authentic expression of who God created him to be.

So when we ask questions like, "What is success?" and, "What is winning?" we have to remember that real success is living out our best, believing we are God's best version of ourselves. Rather than being disappointed by our personal limitations or operating in failure because we don't happen to be the best in the world, we need to stop comparing ourselves to everyone else. Instead, we should look at God's special design as it pertains to us alone. At the end of the day, success is not something we achieve; it's something we live within, an attitude we develop. The apostle Paul reminds us in Colossians, "Whatever you do [whatever your task may be], work from the soul [that is, put in your very best effort], as [something done] for the Lord and not for men" (3:23 AMP).

I'm confident God isn't as concerned with *what* we are doing as he is with *how* we are doing it. Success is a filter through which we see life, not a destination. We live this way by actively and intelligently living in a way that pleases God—doing our best with his best, ourselves.

The lie the enemy often uses to manipulate us into a performance mind-set—one that focuses on the approval of others over the approval of God—sounds like: "You can't just *do* your best; you must *be* the best." Don't get me wrong. I'm all for succeeding and winning gold medals. If your personal best leads to personal victories, then by the grace of God, go for it! But let's not chase our tails simply because the world says we should.

One of the best weapons we have against the enemy here is embracing our identities in him—becoming the people God made us to be. We defeat the enemy when we come out of hiding and leave perfectionism and disappointment behind. Winning in the everyday is about leaning into our calling—nothing more, nothing less. The enemy hates it when we choose to live freely in ourselves.

Remember the lie the enemy told to Eve? His question insinuated: *How God made you and what he offered you wasn't his best.* The lie is so simple, but we fall into his trap if we aren't aware of his schemes.

Setting Intention

My husband and I have been married for twelve years. When I met Ben, I was twenty-five. I was single and ready to mingle. Honestly, I was ready to marry. Then there was a moment in our relationship when love began to grow, and the ember of love eventually grew into a hot passion for each other. Help me, Jesus! Our first year of marriage brought on pregnancy, and I was in labor for our first anniversary. Oh, the joys of life! Five years later I was giving birth to our fourth and final son. All God's people said, "Amen!"

I would love to say that from the first moment we said, "I do," it has been the easiest, breeziest romance. Nope. Not today. Not any day. Most days have been work, harder than I anticipated. Apparently I thought I was marrying myself.

Weird! But for all our effort, we've created a lo'
and fun marriage, and it's been so worth it.

Each time I attend a wedding now and see that look or
young love in the couple's eyes, my mind wanders back to
the day I felt those intoxicating feelings for Ben. There is
nothing like falling in love for the first time. Weddings
also remind me of my lifelong commitment to Ben, to
stand by him through thick and thin. On our wedding
day, we entered into a covenant with God and with
each other, which was witnessed by all of our incredible
friends. That memory causes a rush of love and affection.
I remember to see Ben. Love him. Choose him. I remember my intention.

When it comes to the struggle in spiritual warfare, we
must always go back to God's good intention. The original
question the serpent planted in Eve's heart before she
stepped into sin cast doubt on God's good will toward us.
We have little ability to stay empowered if we don't settle
in our hearts the truth about God's intention. Intention
means purpose. If we understand God's deep love for us,
then when he says something, we will not question his purpose or good intention toward us.

Sometimes when we're in the middle of an everyday
battle and we think about Scripture's warnings about the
work of Satan, it's easy to feel weighed down. However, if
we read through John 10:10 with clarity about God's intentions, we will see Jesus isn't saying, "Watch out. Be very
scared. Dread a life with an enemy in it." No! It's more like:
"I'm going to give you some hard and real facts, but only for

the purpose of keeping you in the sweet spot of life—a life I came to give you." Let's read this verse together:

> The thief comes only in order to steal and kill and destroy. I came that they may have and enjoy life, and have it in abundance [to the full, till it overflows]. (AMP)

God's intention in this verse isn't only to expose our enemy, but also to reveal the wonderment of life. He came to give us a magnificent life—a life we never could have dreamed of.

Looking at Ben through the eyes of intention is what it looks like to see the battle through the eyes of this abundant life. When I see the point of the quest, I'm more prone to fight for it. The promise becomes stronger than the process.

If we discover we have lost our desire to fight, to contend for the life we want to have, then somewhere along the way we have forgotten God's intention. We've grown preoccupied with the battle itself and lost sight of the purpose and the promise at the end. If the battle becomes the focus, who wants to fight for the sake of fighting? I don't. If life is just about the fight, then I'd rather close the door to my spiritual life and go home.

But in moments when I see my future grandchildren in my mind's eye, when I envision growing old with my wonderful husband, when I focus on the four powerful men we are raising together who I believe will change their world more than we could ever imagine, it's at those moments I understand it. My spirit leaps out, and I'm once again infused with strength. I see *zoe*—the abundant life.

I think that's pretty amazing. Don't you think so? When I keep my eyes trained on these things, I'm encouraged to hold fast and keep going. I'm renewed and reminded that the fight really is worth fighting.

EMPOWERMENT POINTS

- God will always see past our lack, past our pain, and speak to the person we are becoming.
- Living a spiritually authentic life is your responsibility alone.
- The epicenter of this battle is within our souls, because our souls are continually in the process of being transformed.
- Real success is living out our best, believing we are God's best version of ourselves.
- Success is a filter through which we see life, not a destination.
- If we discover we have lost our desire to fight, to contend for the life we want to have, then somewhere along the way we have forgotten God's intention.

Chapter 4

An Angel with a
God Complex

I was sick again. Waking up from a deep sleep, I stumbled to the bathroom and threw up over and over. I couldn't believe how quickly this illness had come on. My whole body was now drenched in sweat. I staggered to the sink, washed my face, and muttered to myself in the mirror, "How long is this going to go on?" Feeling overwhelmed, I collapsed back into bed and tried to get a little more sleep. Ready or not, I had an early morning call time to lead worship, and I was going to be there.

At one point in my life, situations like this became typical. A sickness would start slowly, and I would then become violently ill. At first I assumed it was a virus I picked up from one of the kids, since having a large family is like having a kennel. Eventually, everybody gets whatever is going around. But Ben was concerned. He requested I call my doctor to see if he would run some tests, so I reluctantly made an appointment. The following week I went in and they began lab work. After several ultrasounds, multiple medications, and numerous doctors' visits, we ended up back where we started. No answers. My symptoms, though unpredictable, continued.

Then everything came to a halt. I had just finished leading worship for our first service and was preparing for our second one when, all of a sudden, my body began to sweat. I was getting sick again. I ran to the bathroom, knowing my worst fear was happening. My sickness was showing up at the worst possible time, and I had no control. It was terrifying. I quickly washed my face, pulled myself together as best I could, and walked out once again to lead.

Driving home that day, I explained to Ben what had happened to me. I told him that I no longer thought I should lead anything until we figured out what was going on with my body. We joked about me getting sick on stage and how that would change a lot of people's lives, but not for the better. The joking only covered up the deep frustration and sadness I felt when I thought about having to stop everything. I loved what I did. The thought of stopping was especially difficult since we didn't have any answers or a real timeframe. I felt powerless about what was going on.

Desperate, I asked anybody I could for prayer and advice.

Surely someone would have an answer. As I talked with another leader one day, asking for his thoughts and explaining the copious amounts of tests, medication, and rest I was giving myself, he suggested I call an old friend of ours who was particularly gifted in understanding the supernatural. "Maybe it's a spiritual thing." I laughed to myself, wondering how I had forgotten to ask God for answers. Maybe God wanted to show me something.

I hadn't spoken to this particular friend in years. Pulling out an old number, I called and left a message, quickly explaining I needed some counsel. I felt a little strange about the random call, but my desperation overrode any awkwardness. I knew his travel schedule kept him extremely busy, so I didn't expect to hear back from him right away.

An hour later, as I was sitting in the Costco parking lot with two sleeping kids, my cell phone rang. My friend asked me what was going on, and I told him. He listened. After my spiel, with a calm, reassuring voice, he said, "Havilah, I'm getting a picture. You see, sometimes God shows me a picture. I don't know what it means or what it relates to, but sometimes the person I'm talking to does. So I'm just going to tell you what I see, and you can tell me if it means anything. Okay?"

I agreed. I was desperate for help, even if it came in picture form.

He continued, "I see you sitting in an office. There's a man sitting at a desk right in front of you, talking with you."

Immediately a picture formed in my head of an old church office where I used to work.

He went on: "I see you sharing something with him. Does any of this make sense? Do you know what I'm talking about?"

Strangely, I knew precisely what he was describing. "Yes, it does. I'm in our church office with one of my leaders."

"You're sharing something with him, and he is saying something back to you. Do you know what he is saying?"

As if the scene of a movie were playing out, I had an intense feeling of déjà vu. I knew exactly what he was talking about. Tears formed in my eyes, and my voice cracked as I answered, "I'm explaining to the man that I feel called to travel and preach around the world. I feel a deep sense of calling for high impact." Now I was crying in the car.

My friend on the phone asked me, "Do you remember what the man said to you?"

I couldn't believe it. The memory was getting clearer. "Yes. He looked at me and said, 'Well, I don't see anyone else inviting you to come, so just do a good job with what's in front of you.'"

At that moment, my heart and head were in conflict. What the man had said in the office did not sound particularly harsh or hurtful, but I was now full-on crying and didn't know why. Something was being unearthed, and God was trying to reveal it to me.

My friend on the phone said, "Havilah, I want you to think very carefully. What did you say to yourself after this man said this to you?"

I was so overcome by this point, I found it nearly impossible to speak. I did my best to squeak out, "I—I said, if I don't do a good job here, then I guess—I guess my destiny is over." I melted right there in the car. The front of my shirt was soaked with tears, and my eyes fogged up from my running mascara.

The voice on the other end said, "Havilah, you have allowed witchcraft into your life." The word *witchcraft* woke me from my emotional fog. I sat straight up in my seat, concerned. *Witchcraft* had always been a word that represented Ouija boards, tarot cards, and fortune-tellers in our home. We didn't throw this word around lightly.

I said, "I'm sorry, but what do you mean by *witchcraft?*" I could barely hide the concern in my voice.

"Well," he said, "it sounds like there might have been some manipulation going on here, and manipulation is rooted in witchcraft. You can see it in how the situation played out. The moment that man said those words to you, you made a decision in your heart. You decided that if you didn't do a good job, then you would not have a future. At that moment you began to serve this man more than God. You decided to serve this church more than God's purpose. Your performance was more important to you than what God saw in you."

His word, this truth, was like a punch in the spiritual gut. I couldn't believe I hadn't ever seen this in my life until that moment. After all, I was a pastor. I was a leader. Shouldn't I have known? But the shock couldn't overcome the reality of what I was experiencing. Deep down, I knew he was right. God was revealing something that had long been hidden.

The Bible calls these moments *kairos*, the Greek word for "time." Paul used the term when he wrote to the Colossian church. In Colossians, we see Paul explaining something so profound it will make you want to shout amen: "Walk in wisdom toward those who are outside, redeeming the time" (4:5 NKJV).

Kairos would be better translated here as the word *opportunity*. Paul reminds us that we can "redeem the time" or "redeem the opportunity" if we are willing to take advantage of our *kairos* moment. If we are ready to leverage the opportunity, the time we have lost can be redeemed. This means God will help us recoup, recover, regain, and retrieve the time we have given away. But first we have to accept what God is revealing.

I had a choice in my *kairos* moment in the Costco parking lot: to accept or deny what God was bringing to light in my life. Acknowledging what God is trying to say to us is vital for significant and tangible growth. The choice, the next move, is always ours.

Yet when God brings something to light, we can struggle with making the next necessary move toward redemption. Oftentimes it's because we're weighed down with condemnation instead of conviction—and there's a big difference between conviction and condemnation. At the moment the Spirit of God brings clarity and understanding, the enemy would love nothing more than to bring confusion in the way of guilt and shame. He wants to abuse our moment of certainty and twist it so we cannot get free. This is called condemnation.

The moment we recognize this lie of the enemy is the moment we take a step toward freedom. We must choose to accept what God brings to light, reject the condemnation the enemy is trying to place on us, and learn to replace the lie with the truth. Otherwise, we may be putting ourselves in danger. In fact, the Bible says we are even more at risk than before.

> When a corrupting spirit is expelled from someone, it drifts along through the desert looking for an oasis, some unsuspecting soul it can bedevil. When it doesn't find anyone, it says, "I'll go back to my old haunt." On return, it finds the person swept and dusted, but vacant. It then runs out and rounds up seven other spirits dirtier than itself and they all move in, whooping it up. That person ends up far worse than if he'd never gotten cleaned up in the first place. (Luke 11:24–26)

Consider this simple analogy: If you go to the doctor and the doctor gives you a diagnosis, you're partly done with your treatment. If your doctor diagnoses you but doesn't give you a treatment, then you will not be well. Knowing you're sick and understanding your symptoms is only half of the process. Treatment is the first step on the road to getting well. Similarly, this scripture is saying that if we experience a moment of clarity from the Holy Spirit and see the lie exposed, we are only halfway there. We still have to journey toward truth.

Now, back to the story. I asked my friend what I should do next.

"Havilah, if you would like, I can lead you in a prayer that will bring you back into alignment with the Holy Spirit. Would you like to do this?"

I felt another surge of emotion. I blurted out, *"Please!"*

He continued, "Say this after me: 'God, I want to ask your forgiveness for allowing witchcraft in my life. Forgive me for putting what this man said over what you said about me, for believing my performance dictates my purpose. I want to break up with the lie that says anything or anyone can control my destiny over your plans. Will you forgive me? I replace that lie with your truth—the truth that tells me you hold my future. You are not looking for perfection. My destiny will continue whether my performance is perfect or not. I give you back full authority over my life. I am putting you and your opinion above all others. In Jesus' name, amen.'"

I repeated his words as best I could. I was sobbing on the outside, but on the inside I felt a complete and utter breakthrough. The Spirit of God was washing away all of the anxiety, all of the worry, and all of the fear, and he was returning me to confidence.

By then it was raining outside, and I could see the water running down my car windows. The Holy Spirit spoke to my heart at that moment and said, "Havilah, just as this car is being cleansed by the rain, I am raining on you and cleansing you from the inside." It's hard to put into words how different I immediately felt. A huge weight had lifted off my shoulders. I was clean. I felt free!

And you know what? I was free, because after that moment, I was never mysteriously sick again. Only God could do something that supernatural. He set me free from the plans of the enemy.

> Let God work his will in you. Yell a loud *no* to the Devil and watch him scamper. Say a quiet *yes* to God and he'll be there in no time. Quit dabbling in sin. Purify your inner life. Quit playing the field. Hit bottom, and cry your eyes out. The fun and games are over. Get serious, really serious. Get down on your knees before the Master; it's the only way you'll get on your feet. (James 4:7–10)

Understanding Your Enemy

Practically speaking, if we want to recognize the lies of the enemy and turn toward truth, we must learn to understand the enemy and how best to fight against his schemes. I love what T. D. Jakes says about this: "You must understand your enemy, for you cannot defeat what you do not understand."[1]

In the book of Ephesians, Paul gives us one of the most foundational verses to help us understand our battle with the Devil:

> This is no afternoon athletic contest that we'll walk away from and forget about in a couple of hours. This is for keeps, a life-or-death fight to the finish against the Devil and all his angels. (6:12)

Our winning and losing in the everyday will depend on our understanding of the battle and of whom we are fighting. We won't be powerful over the enemy until we see this life-or-death fight up close and personal. We must learn how he operates, uncover his schemes, and acknowledge his threat on our lives, our families, our relationships, and our generation. But seeing him clearly doesn't mean we have to then live in fear. Rather, we can choose to let that clarity aid us in our resistance. The moment we see him as he is—a thief, a killer, a destroyer, an accuser, and an enemy of God—his deception is exposed, and we can begin our journey to defeat him.

Remember, our enemy will always overplay his hand. He is so eager to dominate and control this world that he leaves little to the imagination. He is sneaky, but he is not invisible. He is evil, but he is not all-powerful. He is devious, but the truth exposes him each time. He may surmise what is going on in our lives, but he can't read our minds. Only God can do that.

The apostle Paul had a lot to say about battling the enemy, and his words were not spoken passively. He gave us the straightforward, critical instruction we need to live successful lives. In 2 Corinthians, he encourages us "to keep Satan from taking advantage of us; for we are not ignorant of his schemes" (2:11 AMP).

The truth is, we need to be diligent about our fight against the enemy, because he wants to take advantage of us. Let Rick Renner, a Greek scholar, give you a little more context:

The word *advantage* in this verse is the Greek word *pleonekteo*. This word means *to outwit; to trick; to take advantage of someone through some sinister or sneaky means* . . . [It] denotes a desire to have more, more, and more. It is a form of the word *pleonexia*, the Greek word for *greediness.* In this case in Second Corinthians 2:11, it pictures *someone whose lust for something is so intense that he will take any actions required to obtain what he wants.*[2]

The enemy is not content with those he has under his control. He wants to dominate every person on the earth, including each one of us. The Devil is greedy. He's excessive, eager, and compulsive. He works day and night to trick us and take advantage of us. He is vicious and mean. He is the greatest accuser, abuser, manipulator, deceiver, and controller. He will stop at nothing. His lust is so intense he'll do whatever it takes to get what he craves. His goal is to take us with him into eternal damnation. To do so would be his only win.

But, as Paul pointed out, "we are not ignorant of his schemes." I have often heard the phrase, "Ignorance is bliss," which suggests that if I don't know something, then life is more comfortable, easy, and peaceful for me. But ignorance is not a godly way of thinking. Being ignorant of the enemy's schemes only leaves us vulnerable to his tactics.

Being spiritually illiterate doesn't mean the enemy will leave us alone. It means we are more likely to make critical mistakes due to a lack of full understanding. Ignorance will hurt us and leave us confused, dejected, and deceived. God did not call us to be spiritually blind; he called us to be spiritually alert.

> Stay alert. This is hazardous work I'm assigning you. You're going to be like sheep running through a wolf pack, so don't call attention to yourselves. Be as cunning as a snake, inoffensive as a dove. (Matt. 10:16)

The only way for us to get serious about our eternal fate is to see the Devil as our literal enemy. The Devil is out for blood at any cost. But don't worry: The battle has been won, and we have the advantage. We just have to see him clearly and keep him in his place.

Angel with a God Complex

You may think of God and the Devil as equal and opposing figures fighting each other from two different sides, much like the cartoon image we have of a devil and an angel perched on someone's shoulders. But we need to be clear: The story of God and the Devil isn't one of two gods fighting each other. The Devil is an angel with a God complex. His power and authority are only in his possession because God has allowed him to continue for the time being.

The Devil thought he had won when Adam and Eve ate the fruit in the garden of Eden, but God outsmarted him. Only God could create the redeeming story of the cross. When the enemy could only see Adam and Eve in their sin,

God saw them standing at the foot of the cross completely restored. The enemy saw the end, but God saw the whole story.

I want to take a few minutes to expose the truth about our enemy. Here's Rick Renner's interpretation of the word *devil*:

> The word "devil" comes from the Greek word *diabolos*, an old compound word that is made from the words *dia* and *ballo* . . . The first part of the word is the prefix *dia*, which means *through* and often carries the idea of *penetration* . . .
>
> We've already seen that the devil is looking for an *entry point*. Once a point has been located through which he can secretly slip into people's lives, he begins penetrating the mind and emotions to drive a wedge between those individuals and the other people in their lives. *The enemy's objective is to separate them from each other with his railing, accusing, slanderous accusations.*[3]

These words make me want to shout, jump up and down, cry, and pray—all at the same time. Why? Because I see the Devil relentlessly doing this to every human soul. The enemy's accusations relentlessly penetrate the hearts of his victims. The fearful continue to be fearful. The anxious continue to have debilitating anxiety. The Devil is persistent in his pursuit to render us powerless, to prevent us from stepping into our God-given authority and power.

Have you ever noticed you never struggle with something

just once? Most of us, if we are honest with ourselves, can see the same places of vulnerability year after year. Unless we've had a supernatural breakthrough, we fight the same battles over and over.

But let me say it again: The Devil isn't a god. We are not collateral damage, caught between two different gods as they fight against each other. No! Remember, the Devil is an angel with a God complex. He has mastered the art of faulty power, an optical illusion of his strength.

Growing up, we had a dog named Finney. My dad had an obsession with former revivalists, so most of our dogs were named after them. Finney was named after the leader of the Second Great Awakening, Charles Finney. Finney was a sheltie. He was a little dog, about fifteen pounds. Because maternal hormones raged in our home, he was used to being held all the time. But Finney had a complex; he believed he was as big as every other dog. He was notorious for running up to large neighborhood dogs and starting fights.

One day on a walk we passed a home where a ferocious dog lived. Finney ran up and began to bark. In an instant, Finney disappeared through the slats of the gate and began to attack the other dog. We stood there defenseless, helpless, screaming his name. After the most agonizing sixty seconds, Finney ran back out, beaten up, bleeding, and hurt. Then we carried our dog home. This was just one of many events when Finney started something he didn't have a chance of finishing. We humorously diagnosed Finney with "little-dog syndrome." He was so deceived about his stature that he took on big dogs to prove his strength. This became Finney's great demise.

Satan has the same tendency. He is so filled with pride that he puffs himself up, hoping we believe he carries the same authority and power as God. All of his plans are meant to deceive and control. If we don't understand the power and authority God possesses, we will be caught up and distracted by the enemy's lies.

The Devil may be weak, but he is not stupid. He works the same areas over and over, looking for any opportunity to pick us off. He is unwavering. He sustains his direct attack, his pace, and his intensity.

Ephesians 6:11 says, "Put on the full armor of God [for His precepts are like the splendid armor of a heavily-armed soldier], so that you may be able to [successfully] stand up against all the schemes and the strategies and the deceits of the devil" (AMP). The King James version says, "Put on the whole armour of God, that ye may be able to stand against the wiles of the devil."

The word *wiles* is taken from the word *methodos* in Greek, and it literally means "a road." The Devil is like a traveler who travels on a road. He is headed in one direction and has one destination.

Your enemy isn't wandering around looking for something to do. He's not wasting time. He has a very clear direction and knows exactly where he is headed. His method? To journey on the same path, to the same destination, over and over again in your life. Walking the same path, hoping for an opportunity.

The best part of Ephesians 6:11 isn't the part about the "schemes and the strategies and the deceits of the devil." No, it's the part where Paul reminds us that we have the ability to stand up against him and win.

Is the Devil evil? Yes.

Does he try and attack us even if we have the advantage? Yes.

But he won't succeed if we stand our ground and keep to the promise of victory. With God's authority, we will be able to stand against anything he throws our way.

EMPOWERMENT POINTS

- Acknowledging what God is trying to say to us is vital for significant and tangible growth.
- We can "redeem the time" or "redeem the opportunity" if we are willing to take advantage of our kairos moment. If we are ready to leverage the opportunity, the time we have lost can be redeemed.
- The Devil is an angel with a God complex. He has mastered the art of faulty power, an optical illusion of his strength.

Chapter 5

Satan Comes to Steal

*O*ur camp leader called an emergency meeting in the lobby of our missions base. We had been busy saying our goodbyes, since today was the day we were all headed home. Surprised by the sudden announcement, we wondered if something had happened. We ran up the stairs and through the lobby doors to find four suitcases lying on the floor, opened right in front of us. Some of the contents were still in the suitcases, but other things had been pulled out and laid next to them.

A couple of leaders were standing there, and we were taken aback to see one of our friends there too. Her eyes were downcast. She didn't look up as we walked in. She hadn't been crying, but she seemed distressed.

"Do any of these things belong to you?" one of the leaders asked.

We looked down at the piles of clothes, different shampoos and conditioners, perfumes, makeup, and other assorted items. As we scanned the collection, we began to notice familiar things—things we each had brought to camp for our two-month stay.

We were all a bit stunned. How did our things get in her bags? We each confirmed we had items in this pile, then we looked up at the leader, very confused. He explained that our teammate, our friend, had taken these items from us. He asked that we gather the things that belonged to us and head back to our dorm.

The whole scene was a bit surreal. Still confused, we quickly gathered our stuff and ran back to our room, where we huddled together and talked about how disrespected we all felt.

The focus quickly shifted to our friend. Were we bewildered? Yes. But more shocking was the reality that she came from a very wealthy home. All summer long she had worn new things; her bags were full of clothing with the tags still on them. Each week her parents would send packages to camp with new items for her. Our friend wasn't deprived of anything.

So why did she need to take our things? Unlike her, we didn't come from privileged families. Most of us had saved up all year long to bring what we had. We didn't have tons to choose from like she did, so why would she want our things? Eventually, the truth came out.

Our friend was prosperous, but she was also a thief. She didn't steal because of need; she stole because of want. Stealing made her feel powerful, and she couldn't understand that she was taking our little, even though she had a lot. She craved and took, again and again, until she was exposed.

We might have understood someone taking something because she was needy and had no ability to get it for herself. It wouldn't have made it right, but it would have been understandable. But thinking about someone stealing for entertainment, for the power of being able to do it—that made us feel betrayed and violated.

When the enemy operates in our lives, he is stealing from us as well. We may not realize it as it's happening, but eventually we feel the sense of loss and see that what is rightfully ours has been taken from us. Remember the words Jesus used to describe Satan's work? "The thief comes only in order to steal and kill and destroy" (John 10:10 AMP). So if we want to walk in daily victory, we must remember that the enemy comes into our lives as a thief.

Bump and Lift

Anyone who regularly travels overseas knows about pickpockets. I've bought my share of secret wallets, the kind you tuck under your clothes to wear on various trips. For those who are new to traveling, though, it can be quite a surprise how smoothly pickpockets operate. Oftentimes they're here and gone within a matter of seconds. One technique they employ is called the "bump and lift." A thief will walk in the opposite direction of their victim, coming toward them on a busy sidewalk, for instance, and then intentionally bump into them. The goal is to have the victim focus on the collision while another person, the accomplice, lifts the victim's wallet. The combination of distraction and misdirection gives the pickpockets just enough opportunity to execute the theft.

The enemy of our souls often uses the same technique. Perhaps you have cultivated a joyful attitude, or maybe you're producing fruit of the Holy Spirit. Then the enemy sees your fruit and wants to take it from you.

Have you been growing in faith? He's coming after your belief. Are you experiencing more peace? The enemy will try and take it from you. Not content to sit on the sidelines and watch you become more prosperous, he is possessive and will stop at nothing to own what you have. You will feel the force of his efforts.

Many of us have experienced loss. We have felt the bump of losing a job or of a relationship that's gone sour. Our health may be imperiled, or a medical diagnosis may have rocked our family. The enemy is cunning and smart. He creates opportunities to distract you so he can "lift" your power. He doesn't just demand that you give him whatever you possess. He doesn't simply walk up and say, "Stop believing in God," or, "God's not going to come through." No, he wants to bump and lift you, so you don't even know what's happened until it's done. All of this bumping distracts us;

since the enemy knows this, he takes the opportunity to rob us of our trust in God.

Gift from God

What can we do when our lives are being bumped? How do we keep the enemy from achieving his goal? Though we may not realize it, God has already equipped us to combat the Devil's plan in our everyday lives. When Jesus finished his work on the earth, he left us a part of himself to guide us through these bumpy experiences and lead us into all truth. This part of Jesus is something we've already been discussing: the gift of the Holy Spirit. The Bible says God, Jesus, and the Holy Spirit are all one, but they can also operate independently. The Holy Spirit is the part of God that comforts us, the part that connects our spirits with his. Jesus knew we would need to be encouraged amid the battles of life, so he left us a helper to walk with us through all the bumps:

> These things I have spoken to you while being present with you. But the Helper, the Holy Spirit, whom the Father will send in My name, He will teach you all things, and bring to your remembrance all things that I said to you. Peace I leave with you, My peace I give to you; not as the world gives do I give to you. Let not your heart be troubled, neither let it be afraid. (John 14:25–27 NKJV)

The word *troubled* here is the Greek word *tarassō*, which means to agitate or stir up. The word suggests inward commotion. Imagine someone tossed about by such intense movement that he drops what he is holding.

Jesus warns us that many things in this world are coming to shake us. The shakings of this world will be so intense we may be tempted to drop whatever we are holding. I want to invite you—no, I want to provoke you—not to let the enemy shake you in such a way that you lose sight of what Christ has done for you and within you.

Jesus finished his sentence with this: "Neither let [your heart] be afraid." The word *afraid*, or *deilos* in Greek, communicates a gripping fear or dread, one that produces a shrinking back or cowardice.

Jesus was saying, "I'm coming to bring you peace—a different type of peace that passes your understanding and transcends your mind. Don't let the earthquakes of your life cause you to drop your faith and give the Devil the opportunity to steal it. Don't allow the trouble you're experiencing to force you to shrink back in fear."

You weren't put on this earth to bow down to fear. God didn't call you, save you, and set you apart so that you could live in dreaded anxiety every day. He didn't bring you out of fear so you could return to being a coward. You are strong through Christ. He will make you healthy on the inside if you let him.

The peace Jesus came to give us is not what the world affords. His peace is not an external, circumstantial peace but rather one that comes from an internal and supernatural position. Jesus called himself the Prince of Peace for a reason. He knew we needed this type of leadership, this kind of relationship in our lives.

There is a verse in the book of Isaiah that is filled with this same promise:

> You will keep him in perfect peace,
> Whose mind is stayed on You,
> Because he trusts in You. (Isa. 26:3 NKJV)

You cannot fully understand the gravity of Isaiah's words until you dive into the original meaning. The first Hebrew word I want us to focus on is the word *perfect*. *Perfect* in Hebrew is the word translated *shalom*. Isaiah basically says, "You will keep him in shalom," then adds the word *peace*—the original Hebrew of which is also *shalom*.

Wait a minute. Didn't he already say *shalom*? Is the author stuttering? Did I find the only typo in the Bible?

Not this time. The repetition communicates something entirely different.

He clearly says, "Shalom shalom." Isaiah wasn't trying to create confusion; he was trying to communicate intensity. He was saying, "I will soothe you. I will shalom shalom you—I will usher you into perfect peace when you keep your eyes on me, despite the trouble shaking up your world." God does not want to silence us in our difficulty. Scripture isn't telling us to be quiet about our problems so God can get on with saving the world. Rather, the Spirit of God is coming to rescue us right in the middle of our chaos, to bring us his perfect peace so we will not be distracted by Satan's scheme.

The next part of the verse says, "Whose mind is stayed on You." The word *stayed* means propped up, leaned upon, held up. The picture conveyed is of one object propping up another.

This idea brings to mind one of the most horrific experiences I've ever lived through as a parent. We had just purchased our current home. The two older boys were at school, and my husband was at work. The day was completely ordinary. I had put our two youngest sons in their room to play, so Mommy could quickly finish getting ready in the upstairs bathroom.

Suddenly I heard a scream.

As a mom of four boys, I've learned to decipher particular screams. I've become an expert in "blood screams" and screams that say, "Get off my head." I can discern between "You took my things" or "I need to go to bed." I'm a card-carrying Wail Expert. It's what I do.

This scream sent chills down my back. I instantly dropped my curling iron and ran into the boys' room, but it was empty.

The screaming continued, so I ran through the different bedrooms, looking for my sons. I ran down the stairs through the living room and into the kitchen. As I rounded the corner, I looked through the big glass doors that open to the back patio. Grayson was standing there, banging on the doors. Assuming his younger brother, Beckham, had locked him out, I ran to him. As I opened the doors, I said, "Did Beckham lock you out of the house?"

He looked at me with tears streaming down his face and said, "I fell out of the window!" He was crying hysterically. I picked him up, walked off our porch, and looked up at our second-story window. What I saw next was horrifying. The screen on the window was dangling.

I looked at the ground. Cement was the only place he could have landed. I looked back at his face, and in that moment blood began to pour out of his mouth. I went completely numb. Not wanting to waste a moment, I ran inside and cleared off the kitchen table with one sweep of my hand. I laid Grayson down. I knew enough not to move him in the case of a broken neck, broken back, or internal bleeding. I ran to grab my phone and call 911.

I'd always imagined I would be a calm person when facing an emergency. Most of us have been taught that, while speaking with a medical professional, it's best to stay calm and clearheaded so they can help you. But my mouth didn't get that memo. When the call connected, I frantically began telling the woman on the other end, "My baby fell out of the window . . . my baby . . . he . . . he fell!"

The voice on the other end responded, "I'm sorry, ma'am. You're going to have to speak slower. Tell me again—what happened?"

My face was getting red with anger. I didn't want to slow down. I wanted to yell and scream. I wanted to run through the phone and grab this woman to show her what was happening at my house. I tried again. "Please come to my house. My son. My son, he fell out of the window."

She heard me this time. But she had questions . . . lots of questions.

"Yes, he's breathing . . . um . . . I don't know if anything may be broken . . . Y-Yes, I can keep him awake. Please come quickly, please!"

I stood over Grayson, trying to stay calm. My words did not match my face. I looked into my son's eyes and told him it was going to be okay.

The paramedics came and rushed us to the hospital. When we walked into the emergency room, a team of doctors was waiting for us. They went to work, checking vitals, evaluating his little body, and communicating in medical terms to the team. That's when Ben finally arrived.

Then another request came our way. "Who would like to accompany Grayson to the radiology room? We need to get a full-body scan to see if there's any internal bleeding."

Without hesitation, I grabbed my son's small hand and walked alongside him as they wheeled him down the hall. We entered the CT room and were greeted by the technician.

Looking me straight in the eye, he said, "Okay, Mom, I have two things I need you to do. First, I need you to talk to Grayson. We need to keep him as calm as we possibly can. Second, I need you to grip the back of his neck like this." He put both of his hands under my son's neck with the palms of his hands bracing his head. "You need to keep him as steady as possible. If we can get a good scan, we won't have to do this too many times."

I leaned over Grayson, looking him in the eyes, and I began to talk to him. There's something you need to know. Something you would only learn if you were around the Cunnington family. As I looked at him, I thought of how all of my boys are sumptuously handsome—yet they all look significantly different from one another. Some families are obviously cut from the same mold, but not us. There is only one Cunnington boy, one son, who looks like the spitting image of his mama—and that son is Grayson. Not only that, but Grayson has a raspy little voice like mine as well. We are twins, and he will tell anyone he meets.

So, as I leaned over Grayson, it was like looking into my own face. His eyes were swollen. He was both staring at me but not staring at me because he was in shock. Bloodstains ran down his face and onto his body. Cradling his head with my hands and firmly holding it in place, I said, "Grayson, it's going to be okay. Sweetheart, the doctor is going to help you. You're doing a great job."

Grayson went into the machine and came back out, then back in again and out again. On our third attempt, as I held his head and spoke to him, I saw a change immediately coming over his body. It was as if life was coming back into his eyes. Grayson was coming back! The terror had left his face. I felt him take a deep breath, and his whole body exhaled before completely relaxing.

We covered Grayson again with a warm blanket and took him back to the original room to wait for the results. Fifteen minutes later the doctor entered the room, holding the results in his hand. He said, "Well, I have good news.

There's nothing wrong with Grayson. The blood you see is a bad cut on his tongue, which happened when he fell out of the window. You are all very lucky! You're welcome to gather your things and head home."

What?! I was stunned. We were all stunned. What a miracle. A real miracle!

I wanted to look at the doctor and say, "What?! Well . . . Grayson can go home, but I'm staying here. I would like a bed and maybe some drugs." Of course I didn't say that, but I wanted to.

Ben and I took Grayson to the car with tears streaming down our faces. We stopped in the parking lot, held Grayson in our arms, and made him eat a sandwich.

Then we said two things aloud: "God, thank you for one more day with Grayson." We knew we hadn't been promised anything beyond the moment we had right then. Every day is a gift, and though I didn't like being reminded of it in such a terrifying way, I knew it was the truth. Then I looked at my boy and said, "You are not allowed to come here next year!" I was laughing. "We have to be fair and spread out the deductible between you and your brothers."

This incident comes to mind when I read the prophet's words in Isaiah. Isaiah promised that God will keep us in perfect peace when our minds are stayed on him. As I remember leaning over Grayson, speaking to him, holding his head steady, and looking into his eyes, I remember this too: The Holy Spirit tells me, "Havilah, this is exactly what I'm doing with you. In the midst of chaos, in the midst of the storm, in the middle of the bump, I want to hold you steady. Not only do I want to keep you stable, but I want to lean over you and speak words that will soothe your mind, your heart, and your emotions. I want to prop up the parts of you that seem shaken at this very moment." And that's exactly what he does.

The Devil comes to *shake* you, but God comes to *steady* you. Your enemy comes to "bump and lift" your faith, but the Holy Spirit wants to hold you still, propping you up. God intends to lean over your life and speak gently and firmly about your future, instilling confidence in you once again—all while your eyes stay firmly locked on his.

Seasons of extreme shaking have affected my life so profoundly that I was sure I would drop something—specifically hope. And while I may have lost the momentary feeling of hope, I've never lost hope himself. In those times when nothing but the Spirit of God has held me together, the Prince of Peace has always come to my rescue.

> David, a young shepherd and courageous warrior, the
>   man who became king, said:
> I waited, and waited, and waited some more;
> Patiently, knowing God would come through for me.
> Then, at last, He bent down and listened to my cry.
> He stooped down to lift me out of danger
> from the desolate pit I was in,
> Out of the muddy mess I had fallen into.
> Now He's lifted me up into a firm, secure place,
> And steadied me while I walk along His ascending
>   path. (Ps. 40:1–2 TPT)

God unapologetically loves to keep us steady in the midst of the bumps in life. Like David, we can say the same thing: "Now He's lifted me up into a firm, secure place, and steadied me while I walk along His ascending path." In times like this we get to know a personal, real God who loves us more than we could ever imagine. Satan tries to distract us so he can steal from us, but as we stay our minds on God and wait on him, deep trust is built inside of us and we come to a deep knowing that he will rescue us in times of trouble, in times of hurts, and in times of heartache. We don't need to be worried or afraid of the one who comes to steal from our lives because we have the peace and the strength of the Holy Spirit—the helper Jesus left for this very purpose.

EMPOWERMENT POINTS

- The peace Jesus came to give us is not what the world affords. His peace is not an external, circumstantial peace, but rather from an internal and supernatural position.
- The Spirit of God is coming to rescue us right in the middle of our chaos, to bring us his perfect peace so we will not be distracted by Satan's scheme.
- The shakings of this world will be so intense we may be tempted to drop whatever we are holding.

- The Devil comes to shake you, but God comes to steady you.
- Your enemy comes to "bump and lift" your faith, but the Holy Spirit wants to hold you still, propping you up.
- God intends to lean over your life and speak gently and firmly about your future, instilling confidence in you once again—all while your eyes stay firmly locked on his.
- While I may have lost the momentary feeling of hope, I've never lost hope himself.

Chapter 6

Satan Comes to Kill

My dad was a US congressman's son, but he turned hippie in the late sixties. Looking back on his younger days, he humorously called himself "a long-haired, walking germ." Though his growing-up years seemed charmed from the outside, his story was a tumultuous and broken road. Choices led him to devastating heartbreak, debilitating depression, and eventually suicidal thoughts. After contemplating suicide for six months, he knelt on a beach on a remote Hawaiian island and prayed a prayer out loud. He said, "Jesus, Krishna, Buddha, I don't know which one of you is the real God, but whoever you are, please reveal yourself to me."

Months later he found himself in a small country town

in Northern California called Smartsville. Yes, that's an actual place in California. He ventured into a service at a church, where the man in the front, leading worship on an acoustic guitar, made a straightforward call to the people in the room. He explained the story of Jesus and invited everyone to personally ask Jesus to live in their hearts and change their lives forever.

My dad felt a compelling presence in that moment and accepted the invitation. He invited Jesus to live in his heart and be Lord of his life. But the moment these words left his mouth, the beads he had used to chant to Krishna began to choke him. He was terrified. He said his very first prayer out loud: "Jesus, help me!"

Then he reached up and pulled the necklaces off his throat. The people around him asked what had just happened. He explained what the beads represented, and they told him he had been praying to demons when he used the Krishna beads before. The moment he said his first prayer and cried out to Jesus, he was immediately delivered from those demons.

We must understand how powerful God is in our lives. The moment we invite him to live inside of us, he cleans house. We don't need to be afraid. The demonic powers that have had authority in our lives are forced to leave. Where the Spirit of the Lord is, there is freedom. The enemy is no contest for the power of the Holy Spirit.

My dad's life-changing conversion led him to become an evangelist for the gospel. Living with parents who experienced the supernatural and fought to become people of faith helped forge my own spiritual life. Spiritual battles were never hidden in our home. In fact, my parents talked about their personal struggles many times. They would each describe how the enemy came to bankrupt them. Steal from them. Hurt them. Devastate them.

I knew from a young age that the Devil was real. I knew a battle raged in the heavenly places. Hearing the scripture John 10:10 wasn't abnormal in my house, but it wasn't until I began to study this passage in earnest that I understood how the enemy truly operates.

Let's review the verse again:

> The thief comes only in order to steal and kill and destroy. I came that they may have and enjoy life, and have it in abundance [to the full, till it overflows]. (John 10:10 AMP)

We've spent some time with the word *steal*. Now let's take a look at the Greek word for *kill*. I've heard this scripture a thousand times and always assumed this word meant that the enemy was a killer. Technically, this meaning is right. But that's not the deeper meaning of this passage. Here's what a Greek scholar has to say:

> Jesus said that [the enemy] also comes "to kill" . . . The Greek word is *thuo*, which means *to sacrifice*. It originally referred *to the sacrificial giving of animals on the altar*. It could mean *to sacrifice; to surrender;* or *to give up something that is precious and dear.* It was particularly used in a religious connotation to denote *the sacrifice of*

animals, and it had nothing to do with killing in terms of murder.[1]

When the enemy comes to kill, he hopes you will surrender. He tells you that you have waited too long, believed for too much, and seen nothing happen. You might as well throw in the towel. The crazy thing is, we believe his lies. "God's not coming through for me!" or "We are not going to experience it!" are the enemy's smoke screens.

I've seen this time and time again in the church. Honestly, I've seen this temptation in my own life. The Devil may not have to steal very much from us—especially if we are already giving it away.

I think about the passage where Esau sold his entire birthright for a bowl of soup:

When her time to give birth came, sure enough, there were twins in her womb. The first came out reddish, as if snugly wrapped in a hairy blanket; they named him Esau (Hairy). His brother followed, his fist clutched tight to Esau's heel; they named him Jacob (Heel). Isaac was sixty years old when they were born.

The boys grew up. Esau became an expert hunter, an outdoorsman. Jacob was a quiet man preferring life indoors among the tents. Isaac loved Esau because he loved his game, but Rebekah loved Jacob.

One day Jacob was cooking a stew. Esau came in from the field, starved. Esau said to Jacob, "Give me some of that red stew—I'm starved!" That's how he came to be called Edom (Red).

Jacob said, "Make me a trade: my stew for your rights as the firstborn."

Esau said, "I'm starving! What good is a birthright if I'm dead?"

Jacob said, "First, swear to me." And he did it. On oath Esau traded away his rights as the firstborn. Jacob gave him bread and the stew of lentils. He ate and drank, got up and left. That's how Esau shrugged off his rights as the firstborn. (Gen. 25:24–34)

Esau sold his entire birthright for a bowl of soup. On the surface of things, this may seem plainly ridiculous, but if we're honest with ourselves, we can see how this whole story relates to our generation.

How many of us are giving our bodies away for a moment of pleasure?

How many of us are giving away our character, our integrity, for a moment of entertainment?

How many of us are giving away the babies in our wombs for a moment of ease?

How many of us are giving away our ministries for a moment of fame?

We are selling our birthrights. We are giving away the very breath of God that keeps us alive and motivates us to live an abundant life. We are letting the enemy come in and kill the future God has given us.

Spirit of Fear

I was standing in line for lunch while attending a conference in Los Angeles. I was weeks away from my eighteenth birthday, excited to be exploring my adulthood and finding my grown-up spiritual life. The horizons were new, and I felt anticipation about what God was doing. I felt so full of God's supernatural presence that it was hard for it not to spill over into every conversation.

Then a gentleman next to me began asking questions like, "Where are you from?" and "How did you get here?" I answered him, but quickly I turned the conversation to what God was doing in my life. I shared about my personal encounter with God in the backseat of the car and expressed my excitement to begin living wholeheartedly for him.

He leaned in, listening intently. To my surprise, he responded, "I want to invite you to come on stage and share what God has been doing in your life. I think the whole conference would enjoy your story. How about tonight, right after worship?" I hadn't realized he was connected to the conference, much less that he had the authority to invite me to do such a thing. In my excitement, I quickly agreed.

Then I realized what this guy had invited me to do. His invitation meant standing in front of six thousand people, which, to any normal human being, would be daunting. But as someone with learning issues, it was excruciating. I had avoided public speaking until this point. In English class, I had always been the first to take a zero grade on my speech for nonparticipation rather than receive a reduced grade. I wasn't just nervous. I was terrified.

Feeling inept and limited is normal, but living with learning disabilities takes the phrase "paralyzed with fear" to a whole new level. You end up spending most of your life trying to hide your constraints. It's exhausting.

I spent the rest of that day trying to ignore the approaching evening. I attended the afternoon session and ate dinner with friends. Eventually, we packed back into the auditorium as worship began. The atmosphere was electric, and you could feel a supernatural grace in the room as everyone sang the name of Jesus. It was tangible.

In the midst of this beautiful and glorious moment, the reality of what I was about to do hit me. I began to have a panic attack. Have you ever had one of those? Well, I did. My thoughts raced with questions. *What am I going to do? What am I going to say? I've got to get out of here!*

Running out of the building and around the back, I melted in anxiety. Over the loud singing, I bent over sobbing, trying to catch my breath. My whole body was shaking uncontrollably, and my mind was racing with a thousand thoughts, mostly irrational.

I had completely lost control. I remember telling God in my mind, *You said, "If the Spirit and the Bride say come, you will come." Well, I'm saying, "Come! Like, right now!"* I wasn't joking.

In the middle of my anxious mess, my dad came looking for me. He rounded the corner and saw me bent over in anxiety. Walking up to me, he grabbed my shoulders and looked me square in the eye. What he said forever changed my life.

He said, "Havilah, if you don't look at fear as your enemy, it will defeat you one day."

His words challenged me. He was trying to wake me up from my anxious coma. He was giving me permission to fight back. My racing thoughts came to a halt, and I remember focusing on one clear thought: *I haven't come this far to melt in fear.*

I took a deep breath, pushed my shoulders back, and lifted my head. Gathering all the courage I could muster, I asked the Lord to help me and walked back into the auditorium.

That night turned out to be one of the most defining moments of my life. It changed me forever. It's the reason you're holding this book, the reason I ever wrote a book or spoke on a stage. That very evening, someone heard me share my story and invited me to come to their little church. To a church in a small town named Redding, California—to a small community called Bethel.

Each of us has a personal invitation to live powerfully, to get our fight back. I believe when we find ourselves in a place of paralyzing fear—a place where we either agree with our new identity in Christ or stay the person we've always been, where we choose to walk in the plan God has for us or let Satan take our birthright from us—it's critical to our spiritual health to face our fear head-on.

Strategy

Years ago one of our sons had a debilitating fear. Every night as we would get ready to bathe him, he would scream in horror as we attempted to wash his hair. His fear was so dominant it would monopolize the entire experience. We were at a complete loss. What should have been his favorite time of the day turned into a tangled mess with screaming, wrestling, and frustration.

Exhausted, Ben and I avoided bath time every night until one of us could muster the courage to take on the task. Any parent reading this understands how helpless you can feel. Kids are irrational, so it's impossible to talk them out of fear.

One night, as Ben and I sat in our bedroom, we looked at each other. "We've got to get a plan. We need to help him."

Our son needed a remedy. We understood that if we allowed fear to overcome him, he could battle it for the rest of his life. He needed a game plan. And quite honestly, Ben and I also needed to stop bowing down to this fear and letting it dominate our entire family. It was time to stop living on the defense and get back on the offense.

We walked into our son's room and explained our strategy. "The next time we wash your hair, we want you to say out loud, 'I will not fear!'" We assured him he had permission to say this phrase as many times as he needed. We were commissioning him to use as much force as necessary. We didn't care if he needed to scream or cry; we just wanted him to say it out loud while we washed his hair.

The next day we geared up for bath time, explaining our plan to him again. As we began to shampoo his hair, our son began to scream. We looked at him and said, "Now you can say, 'I will not fear! I will not fear! I will not fear!'"

His little voice started to repeat after us, but it wasn't consistent. "I will not fear (insert terrifying scream). I will not fear."

Ben and I looked at each other as if to say, *We have no idea if this is working, but let's keep going.*

Then he began to say the phrase more solidly. "I will not fear . . . I will not fear!" His hysteria turned into a battle cry. He continued this, night after night, as we bathed him. It didn't take long for the scenario to do a complete turn-around. He was finally free from fear. After that, he never feared washing his hair again.

Like my son, we need a game plan for fear. We need to stop explaining our worry and anxiety away, living as if fear will always be a part of our lives. Paul introduces this promise to Timothy and to each of us: "For God has not given us a spirit of fear, but of power and of love and of a sound mind" (2 Tim. 1:7 NKJV).

When Paul wrote this letter to Timothy, his words clarified how the enemy operates with regard to this particular attack. While the Spirit of God comes in with force to create life, the spirit of fear comes in with force to create death. The enemy uses fear to manipulate, deceive, and control. Until we look at fear as an enemy and a place where the enemy likes to hide, we will never be free.

What does this look like, practically speaking? In a paraphrase of this scripture, Dawna De Silva once wrote, "Fear is dispelled by a powerful recipe of power, love, and a sound mind."[2] Those three elements keep us in courage: the power of the Holy Spirit, the love of our Father in heaven, and a disciplined mind. Each fulfills its role. If we miss one of these ingredients, we wind up with a recipe for fear.

For example, I remember teaching our boys to ride their bikes. The lesson always required a few elements: trust that what seemed impossible (like riding without training wheels) was possible, help from Dad (a good shove and a steady hand) to move them forward, and their ability to use the pedals to continue the forward motion. If one of these ingredients wasn't included, they couldn't ride a bike. If they refused to trust their dad, they would never get on their bikes. If Dad forgot to give them a real push, they wouldn't have enough movement to go anywhere. And if they didn't know how to pedal for themselves, their bike ride would end as quickly as it had begun.

The same is true for us as we combat fear. The foundation of this battle is trusting God's love and intention toward us. When we trust him, we are willing to take risks and believe we can do what God has promised. Then the power of the Holy Spirit moves us forward. He gives us a tangible push toward a lifestyle of faith. Our trust in God and the power of the Holy Spirit then partners with our personal responsibility to discipline our minds. This partnership is where power resides. The three parts work together to keep us out of fear.

The choice between fear and courage is set before us each day. You can either show up and fight or cower in fear. The choice is that simple.

The enemy is real, and each of us is given the opportunity to defeat him personally. To fight him is not a scary proposition but rather the most empowering responsibility of all.

Fighting Fear

I'm the first to say I don't like to fight. Even though I'm outgoing and have an outwardly aggressive personality, I avoid confrontation. In fact, I will do anything to avoid it. I'm like our Goldendoodle dog: a recovering people-pleaser. But warfare is not just for a particular personality type—for those who are aggressive or like to fight. Spiritual warfare is for everyone. The battle is for everyone because we were all meant to win. Succeeding in our spiritual lives is the greatest place of freedom. We were all intended to keep the enemy under our feet. Being powerful is not about personality; it's about a position.

When my dad came to find me that night of the conference, he challenged me to wake up from my anxious coma. Today, I want to challenge you in the same way. Friend, if you don't look at fear as your enemy, it will defeat you. Fear doesn't stay where it begins. Fear will infiltrate every area of your life, paralyzing you until you live a small, worry-filled, defeated life, having surrendered the plans God had for you from the beginning.

Your enemy isn't messing around. He doesn't allow little fears to stay little. He uses our little fears as an entry point for greater fears. His hope is to keep you in spiritual paralysis; he's banking on you cozying up to worry, fear, and anxiety.

Let me remind you: You haven't come this far to melt in fear. You haven't come out of darkness to live in the shadows. You have come out of darkness to live in the light—the light of full confidence in the birthright God has given you. He wants you to have a game plan for fear, a plan to stay stronger than the struggle, a plan to empower you every day with the supernatural strategy of power, love, and a sound mind.

EMPOWERMENT POINTS

- The Devil may not have to steal very much from us—especially if we are already giving it away.
- Each of us has a personal invitation to live powerfully, to get our fight back.
- It's critical to our spiritual health to face our fear head-on.
- We need a game plan for fear. We need to stop explaining our worry and anxiety away, living as if fear will always be a part of our lives.
- Until we look at fear as an enemy and a place where the enemy likes to hide, we will never be free.
- The choice between fear and courage is set before us each day.
- Succeeding in our spiritual lives is the greatest place of freedom.

Chapter 7

Satan Comes to Destroy

I will never forget that night. As we ran into my parents' hotel room, my twin sister, Deborah, and I abruptly woke them up. Through our tears, we gave them the play-by-play of what had happened to us that evening. Twenty-four hours earlier we'd arrived in the city of Tucson, Arizona. My dad had an invitation to minister at a local church, and my sister and I had been squeezed into the schedule for a night of ministry to the youth group. That night was to be our third time ministering to anyone, anywhere. We were amateurs.

But the preparation had begun three months earlier. Actually, it had started the previous year.

We had received a phone call from a friend in Los Angeles named Staci. We had become friends during my high school years when I babysat her kids, and we had kept up with each other afterward through random phone calls and quick visits. Now, God was touching her church community in a profound, supernatural way, and she wanted to know if my sister and I would be open to coming down to see what God was doing. She generously offered to pay for our flights, and Deborah and I eagerly agreed. A last-minute trip to LA? Yes, please. We filled our luggage, hopped on a plane, and climbed into Staci's car less than forty-eight hours after the call.

We had just enough time to make it to the next church service at the conference, and we ran into the auditorium as the first song began. Making our way to our saved seats, I realized Staci had arranged for us to be in the front row. I was not thrilled, but what could I do? I conceded and settled in for the service.

The thought that God was encountering people in a profound way was exhilarating, but I was also skeptical. Deborah and I were a preacher's kids, and preachers' kids are trained to spot phonies. We'd grown up sitting at tables with leaders and hearing stories of church life. We had heard the phone ring at three a.m., visited hospital rooms, attended weddings, and held funerals. Working with real people had been part of our everyday lives. And so we'd grown up cautious. Discerning. Watchful.

As the service continued, I looked up at the stage and assumed we would be experiencing the leading of a gifted, charismatic worship leader. After all, thousands of people were coming to this auditorium, and the only other situations where I had seen packed rooms were under that type of leader. But the guy up on stage was not that. He strummed five chords on his guitar and sang—a simple set with just a few band members and a weak sound system. He would sing and strum, close the song, flip the page, and do it all over again.

For those of you who are part of faith communities used to having start and stop songs done in an orderly fashion, let me just tell you: This is not the charismatic way. Charismatics love music, and they hate silence. The goal in most charismatic worship services is never to allow the person attending to experience silence. The song service should be at least thirty minutes long with no breaks, unless the worship leader, who has been dreaming of being a preacher, takes over in the middle of worship to preach a five-minute message. So this methodical, somewhat quiet worship set was quite different from what I had been expecting, to say the least.

Then the pastor came up to preach his message on evangelism. As an evangelist's daughter, I quickly understood where this pastor was going. At the end of his message, he made an appeal to everyone in the room. It wasn't a salvation call, but it was directed to those who felt led to have evangelistic influence in their communities.

I thought to myself, *Who isn't going to respond to this message? Isn't being evangelistic foundational to being a Christian? It's the easiest altar call anyone can make.* I know . . . I wasn't very nice.

He asked for those who felt they wanted to respond to

the message to come forward for a time of prayer. Three-fourths of the room made their way to the front. Since our friend had strategically placed us in the front row, we were automatically in the altar call whether we wanted to be or not. Standing there, the leader began to ask the Holy Spirit to manifest his presence among us.

I watched a middle-aged woman make her way in front of me. Her hair, makeup, dress, heels, and jewelry were all meticulously planned. She was a picture of perfection. As she lifted her hands, I could tell she instantly began to experience something in a significant way. Almost as if electricity were touching her, she shook and fell to the ground. But there wasn't anyone to catch her. She just dropped onto the hard cement floor, which was barely covered by a thin layer of carpet. She lay there, her eyes closed and tears streaming down her face. She wasn't hurt, and her face didn't reveal fear. In fact, a huge smile crossed her face. She was actually enjoying herself.

At that moment my cynicism began to change. I felt my heart opening up to what God was doing in the room. Staci came over to me, gently laying her hand on my shoulder, and began to ask the Holy Spirit to minister to me as well. I felt a spiritual lightning bolt, as if something had come from the heavens and shot through my physical body. I didn't know it at the time, but I fell to the ground and began shaking myself. I had no theology for this. I remember thinking, *But I don't even believe this!*

I was experiencing the incredible and tangible presence of God. All the Bible stories, all the altar calls, all the life lessons and prayer times—everything I had believed in faith. Everything I had hoped was true all became real to me. I felt the presence of God as I had never felt it before. He wasn't some far-off, distracted, and distant God. No! He was real. He became as real as the hand in front of me. This moment forever anchored my life, and I became a different person in a moment. But this was just the beginning of what God was doing at this conference.

Earlier, a guy about our age had come up to my sister and introduced himself, nervously explaining that he was hoping she could pray over him. Deborah was surprised since we were guests and had never seen this guy before. She quickly ran up to me and asked what she should do. We laughed, thinking this might be the way guys pick up girls at conferences these days. Maybe he would ask for us to lay hands on him next? I digress. So she said what every "Christian leader" says to get out of things: "If the Lord leads, then I will find you later." Thus began our days of avoidance. This guy came up to us any chance he could, asking if my sister was ready to pray for him, and she would say, "No, not yet" and quickly go into hiding.

On the last night of the event, we stayed for prayer. The 6,000 people who had attended the conference had slowly trickled down to 150 by then. Only those who wanted to stay late into the evening to pray remained. When one a.m. rolled around, we gathered our things to leave, but before we could, the same guy tapped Deborah on the shoulder. "Can you pray for me now?" She was caught red-handed. It was evident we were not coming back tomorrow, so this was his moment.

So she grudgingly agreed, asking Staci and me to join her. We gathered around him. He closed his eyes and stretched his hands out in front of him, ready to receive. His face glowed with eagerness, but I was annoyed.

We began to pray, and almost immediately Staci said out loud, "Havilah, I think you have something for him. I think God has given you something to tell him."

I looked at her in utter shock. First, I couldn't believe she thought I could hear anything from God for this guy. But second, I couldn't believe she had called me out, and now everyone around the circle was looking at me.

I'm sure she could see the shock on my face, so she quickly said, "Havilah, just close your eyes and say the first thing that comes to you."

I closed my eyes, but the first thing I thought about was McDonald's fries. Let's be honest: I was a seventeen-year-old, and it was one thirty in the morning. I don't know any teenager who wouldn't want McDonald's fries at that time of night. I'm not sure we ever outgrow this craving. But I knew that wasn't this guy's word from the Lord, so I kept my eyes closed and waited.

All of a sudden, like a photograph that's been dipped into developer chemicals causing the image to quickly appear, I heard the name *Meshach*. I instantly knew who this man was from the Bible. Do you remember the three people who were thrown into the fiery furnace because they wouldn't bow down to King Nebuchadnezzar? Well, one of them was named Meshach. My brain was rapid-firing. I thought to myself, *I know his name is not Meshach. Why would I say that name?* But in predictable fashion, I then thought, *Well, if the word is wrong, this guy deserves it. After all, he's been stalking us for days.*

So I mustered up my courage, and a little cynicism, and said it. "I hear the name Meshach!" I couldn't believe my eyes at what happened next. The very moment I spoke, the guy fell to his knees and began to sob. I was flabbergasted. I didn't know what was happening. Apparently, the name meant something to him, and he knew it. My friends joined in, sharing what they felt God was saying. After a few more words, he picked himself up, wiped all the tears from his puffy face, and flashed a huge smile.

Some of his friends had gathered around him as we prayed, and when he picked himself up off the ground, he put his arm around one of his buddies. He looked at the three of us and said, "Can you pray for my friend too?" This guy was not afraid to ask. Relieved by what had just taken place, we joyfully accepted the challenge.

His friend stationed himself in the same manner: eyes closed, hands out in front of him, face tilted toward the heavens, and a smile strung across his face. He was clearly expecting something to happen. We closed our eyes and began to pray.

Staci, without hesitation, again said, "Havilah, I think you have something for this guy too."

I thought, *I'm sorry, what? Are you seriously going to ask me to give another word? I have a twin sister standing right next to me. Pick her! You've probably gotten us mixed up. Most people do.* But as I eyed her with a questioning look, she confidently nodded at me as if to say, *Go ahead. You've got this!* I closed my eyes and conceded.

This time I was a little more ready. As I stood there with my eyes closed, another name surfaced—*Shadrach! Are you serious, God? Did you give me another name? Not only that, but you're giving me a name from the same chapter of the Bible? God, it's a huge Bible! Couldn't you flip the page and use something else?* Then the critical part of my mind said, *Well, again, even if it doesn't mean anything, these guys might deserve it. We didn't ask to pray for them, now, did we?* So I spoke the name.

The guy had the same reaction: shaking, falling to his knees, and sobbing. What was going on? Did I have the gift of names? Was I renaming these men? I was dumbfounded. But I could feel the presence of God, and I knew these men were having an authentic experience. They were hearing something that only they and God knew about. I wasn't in the know.

At this point, a line began to form—much to our dismay. The second guy picked himself up from the floor, and a third friend was ready for his turn. We closed our eyes and began to pray. I heard the same voice inside of me, which I now know is the Holy Spirit, giving me the name *Abednego*—but this time I was ready. I knew what I had to say. Quickly ignoring my hesitation, I told him, "I heard the name Abednego over you!" The guy crumbled.

One more guy, one more name: *Daniel.* An hour later we were done, and the four guys approached us. Their arms were wrapped around one another, standing in front of us like a band of brothers. The first guy said, "I'm sure you hear this all the time, but your words were spot on. A prophet came to our home church in Alabama. He called each of us out separately in the room. We were not sitting together. He then pointed to us individually, saying, 'You're a Daniel, a Meshach, an Abednego, and a Shadrach.'"

Each of them had already heard these names over their lives before. The fact that God knew them, saw them, and had revealed the same word in a different state and a different church—not to mention with strangers around and from the lips of a seventeen-year-old girl—blew their minds. They were now convinced. Grounded. Grateful.

I looked at them and said without hesitation, "We do. We hear that comment all the time." After all, I was seventeen and enjoyed a little joke. That night Deborah and I could barely sleep. God had shown up in a ridiculous and glorious way.

We went home the next day and shared with our parents what God had done. They were excited. Their greatest dream had been for us to encounter God, but encountering him and simultaneously helping others encounter God—well—their minds were blown.

My dad jumped up from the kitchen table to make a phone call. Promptly returning, he declared, "I got you girls a speaking engagement in Utah! I spoke with the pastor, and he's happy to let you minister to their youth while I speak to the adults." You would think at this point we would have been eager, but instead we were furious. My dad was a minister, so invitations were exciting to him. We were high school students, so invitations were terrifying to us.

On the scale of desire, it was a minus five. We emotionally spilled our concerns. He, being an enthusiastic Italian father, explained that we didn't have to worry because the event was three months away. He was convinced we would gain our confidence by then.

Three months later our family packed up our car in California and drove to Salt Lake City. Deborah and I were in complete denial; we hadn't talked about what we were going to do or how we were going to do it, so we were faking it all the way. When we arrived at the church, the pastor greeted us energetically. "We're so honored to have you all with us! We heard you girls would be speaking tonight to our youth group. Awesome! We were also told you both prophesy. Our young people are really excited."

I want you to understand: Deborah and I had never ministered before or after that night at the conference in LA. We assumed it was a sort of one-hit-wonder moment, and we never believed we'd experience it again. We looked at him in panic, and I quickly said, "Well, we're not sure . . . I mean, I guess if God leads . . ."

The pastor apparently missed the deer-in-the-headlights look we had on our faces. He didn't notice we were trying to avoid our responsibility, or maybe he felt a little challenged. Either way, he quickly and aggressively said, "Well, I sure hope God leads, because we told our youth that this is what you guys are going to be doing. They would be very disappointed if you didn't."

We were speechless. I passed out right then and there. Okay, not really, but I wanted to.

Driving to our host's home, we chastised my dad the whole way. "What would possess you to tell this man that Deborah and I prophesy? Why would you do this to us?" Now, in a regular family, teenage daughters might have found empathy after expressing their anxiety—but for my parents, the more worked up Deborah and I got, the funnier they thought it was. They began to laugh! They said, "Look at you girls. You seem so upset! You will be okay." We were not fine. In fact, we were extremely ticked off.

We were greeted by the same pastor when we returned to the church later that night. He couldn't get the words out fast enough. "Do you girls remember how we said there would be sixty kids here tonight? Well, you're not going to believe it! One hundred and twenty kids showed up. It's a packed house." Talk about the last thing we ever wanted to hear. I thought I was going to throw up.

He then led us to the room where we were going to minister. It was the size of a large classroom, about fifty feet wide. Almost every square inch of the room was filled with chairs and faces. Deborah and I huddled in the corner together to come up with a game plan. "Okay, here's what we're going to do," I said. Deborah grabbed an old piece of paper and a pen to write down the order of things. "You're gonna speak your message. Then I'm going to sing the song I wrote. I'll close out in prayer. We'll wait a few minutes and then shut down the service. I'll make sure to tell the leader we just didn't feel led to prophesy." I wish I was joking, but this is exactly how it went down.

The room was loud, so we could barely hear each other.

We nodded in a "Let's do this!" sort of way, and Deborah opened up the night. She had prepared fourteen pages of a message but was done speaking in seven minutes. Having never preached before, she just read her notes verbatim. She then led the room in prayer, explaining that I would be singing a song next. What I forgot to mention is that the entire sound system had gone out minutes before we began. The temperature in the room was hot due to the number of bodies, so they had put a sort of airplane fan in the back of the room—one of the biggest fans I had ever seen. The sound alone was distracting, but without an amplifier system, hearing my raspy voice and the little speakers coming from the keyboard would have been impossible for the crowd.

Out of sheer willpower, I sang my song. Eyes closed, pounding the keys. It was horrible! I'm sure the enemy looked at me and thought, *I could use this girl!* I could feel sweat dripping down my back, and my heart pounded out of my chest. I couldn't think. I couldn't breathe. I was in an automatic panic. When the song closed, I looked up to see the entire room with their heads still bowed. I hadn't planned on saying this, but nothing was going as planned. "If anyone feels the presence of God, I want you to stand up and come forward."

Clearly I hadn't thought this through, because there was no space for them to come forward in this tiny room. I didn't care. My thought was simple: *I'm not feeling a thing, but if I can find someone in the room who is, I would like to know.* After I made the call, I opened my eyes and saw the majority of the room standing. Different ones began to cry, and I heard sobbing coming from different places. God was at work. Those who had tried to make their way to the front kneeled down. There happened to be no leaders in the room because most of them were listening to my dad preaching in the main auditorium. Deborah and I were almost entirely alone with people of our own age group.

We looked at each other, and I whispered, "Let's begin to pray for them. You take that side of the room, and I'll take this side of the room." And that's what we did. We prayed for them one by one, and God started tangibly touching them. After a few minutes, I looked at my sister across the room. She was praying for a large guy who was about six foot three. She had her hand on his shoulder, and her finger was pointed up toward him. His eyes were closed, and tears were streaming down his face. As her hand moved, her gaze locked in on him. I realized she was prophesying. I thought, *I gotta get over there!* So I stepped on a few people, rushing to where she was.

As she prayed, I began to hear that same voice inside of me—yes, the one I'd heard at the conference. I started to share what I was hearing. The guy broke down again. We then went to the next guy and then the next girl. Each one broke as we shared what God had given us.

One of the youth leaders followed us around with a little tape recorder, recording what we were saying and giving the tape to each student. Person after person, minute after minute, hour after hour, we went on. At the end of the night, he had given a hundred tapes away. It was crazy! God was faithful. We were amateurs, yet he was a devoted Father.

You can imagine our enthusiasm a month later when

we drove into Tucson, Arizona, for what would be our third time in ministry. After our experiences in LA and Salt Lake City, the bar had been set pretty high. But this time wasn't anything like what had happened before. During the service, the youth pastor abruptly interrupted the altar call we were leading, which confused us—but we were young and inexperienced and did not understand what was going on. Later that evening, when he took us out to eat Mexican food, we asked him what he thought of the night. He said, "Honestly, I don't believe in anything you did tonight. I don't believe women should be in ministry. I don't believe in the message you brought. And if I had known what you would do tonight, I never would have asked you to come." We couldn't end the meal fast enough. We were shocked. Young. Immature. Innocent. Crushed.

So after he dropped us off at our hotel, we ran into my parents' hotel room to tell them exactly what happened. My dad looked at me and said, "Well, I guess you get to decide if God called you or man called you." He was right. I felt as if I were inside the movie *The Matrix*. Two pills were being held out in front of me, and I had a choice to make. Was I going to believe what God said or what my enemy said? The decision was that simple.

Unfortunately, the choice may have been simple, but my journey to believing the truth wasn't. After twenty years of sharing that story, I've learned a few things about our enemy. We've talked already about how he comes to steal and to kill. Now let's talk about the third thing he does, as mentioned in John 10:10: He destroys.

The enemy doesn't merely want to convince you to sacrifice God's goodness. No! He wants to ruin your life, trash it so badly that there is no evidence of a miracle-working God anywhere in your story. He would love to see you devastated, living a completely wasted life with no eternal value, every bit of your inner being destroyed.

He does this in a strategic and methodical way. Your enemy is not all-powerful, and he doesn't have the ability to see all things—but he is very patient. He will wait for the most opportune time to destroy what God has genuinely done in your life. He watches you. Studies you. He knows what lies you will believe.

How does he know? Well, usually we tell him! How many times have you said, "If that happens one more time, I'm going to (insert negative action)"? He then takes that nugget of information and tucks it away for just the right time to exploit it. No more, I say! A surefire weapon of warfare is to never let the enemy know what he can use against you. This doesn't mean we can't tell God what we are thinking or reach out to others for help; it just means that because our words carry life, we should not waste them.

A scripture I often read to motivate myself to speak truth is found in Proverbs 18:21: "Death and life are in the power of the tongue, and those who love it and indulge it will eat its fruit and bear the consequences of their words" (AMP). *The Message* version says, "Words kill, words give life; they're either poison or fruit—you choose."

This verse suggests that when we speak words of death or destruction, the only way for the phrase to be challenged or changed is to interrupt it with a life-giving word. When we speak something from a life-or Spirit-filled perspective, the words will take root like living things and continue to grow. When we speak, we are sowing seeds and will reap a harvest. We can speak faith over our lives, believing God can do something and praising him for it. And guess what? Rather than gaining information he can use against us, the enemy has to hear a continual stream of living words in his ears. To him they must sound like clanging cymbals crashing over the darkness.

Declaring

One strategy for speaking faith and life to combat the enemy's destruction is the simple act of declaration. Declaration is pronouncing what you believe rather than what you feel. Did you know that God enabled us to act even before we feel ready? We aren't reliant on feeling something to put it into action, and we don't need to believe something before we say it. In fact, the more we say something, the more we believe it—and then our feelings will follow. Likewise, our minds can't decipher between what we hear and what we think, so when we say something, our minds interpret it as fact. This process is stronger than you know!

Think about it this way: Have you ever woken up exhausted? You have a full day of demands and just don't feel up to it. When someone asks you how you are, you respond, "I'm exhausted." The truth is, the more you say how tired you are, the more you feel it. The opposite can also be true. If you wake up exhausted but say aloud, "I'm doing great!" you will find the capacity to deal with the demands of the day. Mere discipline can be followed by delight.

I remember using this strategy one day when I was feeling discouraged about my relationship with Ben. We were trying to work something out between us and found ourselves in a gridlock. We kept going around and around. I had shared my thoughts and my perspective for many days, and he had too; yet we couldn't seem to get anywhere.

I was feeling defeated when I walked into my bedroom and told God, "I don't know what you want me to do. Ben and I are at a standstill."

All of a sudden, the Holy Spirit whispered to me, "Havilah, begin to praise me for your marriage and the man I gave you. Don't let the enemy know how overwhelmed and helpless you feel. Those are just feelings, but the truth is you're anointed to be in this relationship. I'm going to give you keys and secrets to loving your husband well, and you will get through this."

And that's exactly what happened! I began to walk around my room, declaring the truth and thanking God for my marriage. I said, "Thank you, God, for the man you gave me. My marriage is going to thrive. I can't believe I get to spend my life with Ben. Our life together will only get better! I thank you for giving me a man who loves you and knows you. I thank you that this is just the beginning of the supernatural life we've been called to together." I began to declare what I hoped. Immediately I felt a tangible grace. I walked out of that room a different person. A few minutes earlier I had walked in feeling discouraged, overwhelmed, and defeated; I walked out feeling hopeful, open, and at peace. Nothing had changed on the outside, but everything had changed on the inside through the act of declaration.

I'm not the first person to employ this strategy. Our father Abraham did this exact same thing. Let's look at how the book of Romans tells the story:

> We call Abraham "father" not because he got God's attention by living like a saint, but because God made something out of Abraham when he was a nobody. Isn't that what we've always read in Scripture, God saying to Abraham, "I set you up as a father of many peoples"? Abraham was first named "father" and then *became* a father because he dared to trust God to do what only God could do: raise the dead to life, and with a word make something out of nothing. When everything was hopeless, Abraham believed anyway, deciding to live not on the basis of what he saw he *couldn't* do but on what God said he *would* do. And so he was made father of a multitude of peoples. God himself said to him, "You're going to have a big family, Abraham!" (Rom. 4:17–18)

A strategy for defeating the enemy is declaring truth over your life, declaring in faith what will be. God told Abraham he would be a father of many, so Abraham trusted God to make him just that—even though he was childless for many, many years. Abraham was old and well beyond prime child-fathering years, but it didn't matter; God called him a father. Fact is one thing, but the truth is another. We don't disregard fact, but we aren't relegated to it either. Truth speaks a better word. Truth speaks of God's intention, his plans, his calling. We need not resign ourselves to the facts the enemy points to as evidence of God's unfaithfulness. Instead, we say no to the destruction he tries to sow. Instead, we speak to the mountain standing in our way and declare it will move, in Jesus' name.

Jesus told us about this himself in the book of Matthew when his disciples asked him why they'd failed to cast out a demon.

> "You're not yet taking God seriously," said Jesus. "The simple truth is that if you had a mere kernel of faith, a poppy seed, say, you would tell this mountain, 'Move!' and it would move. There is nothing you wouldn't be able to tackle." (17:20)

Where are most of our mountains? In our minds, our thought life. Our minds are our biggest battleground. What we let happen in our thoughts will come out in our actions. Rick Renner wrote,

> Most of the attacks the devil wages against you will occur in your mind. He knows that your mind is the central control center for your life; therefore, if he can take control of one small area of your mind, he can begin to expand outward into other weak areas that need to

be strengthened by the Holy Spirit and the Word of God. By poisoning your mind with unbelief and lying strongholds, the devil can then manipulate not only your mind, but also your emotions and your body. There is no doubt about it—the mind is the strategic center where the battle is won or lost in spiritual warfare![1]

I would love to say that after that night in Tucson, after I sat and thought about what my dad had said, I never had to deal with insecurity about what that man said to me. I would love to say that I decided to move forward confidently in what God had called me to. But the truth was, I lived with that man's words for a long time.

For many years I would stand up to minister, and, instead of seeing my life from God's perspective or hearing his words as the dominant voice in my life, I would hear the pastor's words ringing in my spiritual ears. I would hear, *"If I had known what you would do tonight, I never would have asked you to come,"* and then these words from the enemy would play over and over in my mind: *If they had known what you were going to bring, they would never have invited you.*

The enemy doesn't have to say it over and over again if we believe it the first time. The narrative in our heads is often something we repeat to ourselves without any help from our enemy. Generally we are the ones responsible for the continual, repetitive messages.

Interestingly enough, no one else ever said those words to me again. It was a twenty-minute conversation that happened twenty years ago, but, for some reason, I have heard those words thousands of times. Why? I kept them alive in my head. When I felt weak or vulnerable, when I felt unappreciated or underutilized, I practiced these words, memorizing them and using them against myself.

We all do this to ourselves. How do I know this? I've seen it happen in thousands of people's lives over the years. Our enemy's greatest strategy is hoping we will use someone else's words about us as ammo. Something is said one time, but we repeat it thousands of times. He hopes we will use simple, damaging words as places to hide fear, shame, feelings of worthlessness, and rejection over the years. Again, where has the enemy come to destroy each of us? In the area that holds the most power: our minds.

The enemy witnessed the moment at the Los Angeles conference when my reality and theology collided. He watched my spiritual confidence grow in Utah. He didn't interrupt those moments. He didn't expose himself or his power because it would have looked weak or humorous in the presence of God. My enemy waited until my defenses were down and I wasn't expecting resistance. He waited until I was vulnerable. Then he used the opportunity to throw fiery darts at me, hoping to destroy my soul.

But the truth is, just because fiery darts have burned us in the past doesn't mean we must live as burn victims forever. In fact, we can fight the good fight of faith, learn to discern moments of danger, and win each time. We might have experienced moments of destruction, but our future is not destroyed.

I'm going to teach you how to win in the next chapter.

We will follow the greatest example given to us on earth: the life of Jesus.

EMPOWERMENT POINTS

- He [your enemy] will wait for the most opportune time to destroy what God has genuinely done in your life.
- A surefire weapon of warfare is to never let the enemy know what he can use against you.
- When we speak something from a life-or Spirit-filled perspective, the words will take root like living things and continue to grow.
- We don't disregard fact, but we aren't relegated to it either. Truth speaks a better word.
- The enemy doesn't have to say it over and over again if we believe it the first time.

Chapter 8

Know the Word

It was the end of the school year, and we were graduating five interns from our local ministry school. The third-year program included an activation year. Any student who applied had the chance to hang out with his or her mentor the following year and glimpse behind the scenes of real-life ministry (aka, "where all the magic happens").

I had signed up to be a mentor and had picked five women to walk with that year—each distinct, each beautiful, each from a different place. During the final week of the school year, I walked into my personal assistant Tiffany's office and hurriedly explained that I wanted to purchase a gift for each of the women I had been mentoring. Specifically, I wanted something that would symbolize their growth that year. A new company had emerged in town that offered handmade jewelry, so we decided to purchase each of my mentees a necklace. We asked that the necklaces be stamped with a personalized message, a truth statement Tiff and I outlined for each woman—words like *fearless*, *brave*, *joyful*, and *passionate*. We knew they would love them.

The final day came, and we were sitting in an elegant restaurant with these women when we handed them their beautiful, personalized necklaces. We celebrated, toasted, took pictures, and said our goodbyes, even though we still had a few more days together the following week.

The next Tuesday came, and Sue, our oldest intern, walked into our office. Sue was a kindred spirit. She'd left her homeland of Great Britain to begin an adventure in the States and had added so much to our ministry: life, energy, and joy despite a personal story filled with heartbreak and pain. She wanted to tell us something, so Tiff and I squeezed into my office, excited to hear what she had to say.

She began, "Do you remember when you gave me that necklace? The one that says, 'Fearless Lover'?"

Of course we did. We'd been so thrilled to call out that quality in her, the way she passionately loved God and had overcome so much fear. We nodded excitedly.

"Well, I loved it! In fact, I put it on immediately and began wearing it. It didn't seem funny to me until I walked into a gas station to get gas the following day. The gentleman helping me at the cash register was looking down at his register when I walked in, but as I began to pay, he looked up. He glanced down at my necklace and then panned back up to my face. I assumed the jewelry had caught his eye. It wasn't until he looked at me with a smirk on his face and said, 'Is it true?' that I realized why he was smiling. My face turned red. The man was asking if I was a fearless lover—and not in the spiritual sort of way."

We gasped. Wide-eyed and covering our mouths, we let out a hysterical laugh. We couldn't believe we had missed this small yet critical detail. Poor Sue! She was a good sport, but to this day it's still one of our favorite stories to laugh about. It's still funny.

I share this story to explain a simple truth: Just because something works in one environment doesn't mean it works in every environment. Some things, some experiences, only translate in a specific place or to a specific person.

Many of us have already learned something about our enemy. We may have read a book on spiritual warfare, attended a conference, or received some teaching and instruction that helped us to understand more. We may have found comfort in a passage or a song during a particularly hard season. But we must realize that, while all those things were helpful in a specific season or place and time, they may not be universally translatable to every situation going forward. We must hold to what *is* going to remain helpful and relevant across seasons, cultures, and experiences: God's truth.

Warfare Techniques

Now, remember: Our enemy is defeated, but we still need to know how to deal with him. The better we understand how he operates, the more powerful we will be at fending off his deceptions. And though we might have gathered some warfare techniques that are unique and personalized to us, such techniques might not make sense to the rest of the world. That's why we're going to focus on some techniques that *are* translatable: timeless truths that are not limited to a certain denomination, gender, ethnicity, temperament, or personality. They work because they are biblically sound. They work because Jesus used them.

These strategies for dealing with our enemy are not secrets you can only learn about after completing some ritual; they live in plain sight in the Scripture God has given us. God did not hide anything from us. He put it out in the open so we would know exactly what to do when struggling with the enemy. You will be well equipped if you can learn these few strategies.

Quick and Specific Words from God

Let's start by visiting some foundational verses. I want to show you theologically and historically how God set us up to win. Ephesians 6:10–17 is one of my favorite passages when it comes to spiritual warfare. When Paul wrote this letter to the Ephesian church, he wrote to help them understand what they were facing.

> Finally, be strong in the Lord and in his mighty power. Put on the full armor of God, so that you can take your stand against the devil's schemes. For our struggle is not against flesh and blood, but against the rulers, against

the authorities, against the powers of this dark world and against the spiritual forces of evil in the heavenly realms. Therefore put on the full armor of God, so that when the day of evil comes, you may be able to stand your ground, and after you have done everything, to stand. Stand firm then, with the belt of truth buckled around your waist, with the breastplate of righteousness in place, and with your feet fitted with the readiness that comes from the gospel of peace. In addition to all this, take up the shield of faith, with which you can extinguish all the flaming arrows of the evil one. Take the helmet of salvation and the sword of the Spirit, which is the word of God. (Eph. 6:10–17 NIV)

There is so much here, but I want to focus on the final portion of the scripture. Paul said, "Take the helmet of salvation and the sword of the Spirit, which is the word of God." "Word of God" was a phrase Paul used often in his letters. In fact, this phrase is used 311 times throughout the New Testament. Its most common Greek equivalent is the word *logos*. *Logos* means the entire written Word of God. It's safe to say this would mean your Bible. If I were to say, "Can you hand me my Bible?" I could replace the word *Bible* with *logos*. They mean the same thing.

Interestingly, though, when Paul commissioned the church to fight the enemy in this passage and urged them to use the Word of God as their sword, he didn't use the word *logos*, as most would assume. Paul used an entirely different word. He used the word *rhema*, meaning a quickened, specific word from the Spirit.

Why would Paul use *rhema* instead of *logos*? The secret is in understanding how Roman soldiers fought in battle during biblical times. Roman soldiers were extremely committed to warfare. They trained under a strict regimen twice a day and became skilled athletes, practicing with swords made of thick wood, twice the weight of the ones used in battle, to build endurance and strength. When the time came to go into actual battle, they used a small sword about the size of a dagger and stabbed quickly and swiftly, saving their strength for the war.

Flavius Vegetius Renatus, who lived around 380 AD and documented the affairs of the Roman military, wrote:

> They [the military recruits] were likewise taught not to cut but to thrust with their swords. For the Romans not only made a jest of those who fought with the edge of that weapon, but always found them an easy conquest. A stroke with the edges, though made with ever so much force, seldom kills, as the vital parts of the body are defended both by the bones and armor. On the contrary, a stab, though it penetrates but two inches, is generally fatal.[1]

The Romans were experts in understanding their opponents' bodies. Since their expertise was stabbing and thrusting with precision, they only needed to plunge their swords in two inches to kill their enemies.

When Paul wrote the words in Ephesians 6, he knew the church would picture a Roman soldier carrying himself as an expert warrior—one always prepared for battle. When Paul wrote, "The sword of the Spirit, which is the word of God," the people didn't envision large swords cutting and slashing. No, they would have pictured small daggers thrusting and stabbing in a lethal manner.

In choosing a term that referred to a quick and pointed word from the Lord, Paul was commissioning the church to fight their enemy with clarity and swiftness. He was saying, "When you fight your enemy, don't take words from your Bible and throw them broadly. Receive a precise word from the Spirit and then take your enemy down quickly. You could say, 'Don't slash your enemy with the *logos*; pierce him with the *rhema*.'"

What does this type of battle look like in daily life? Here's one story that comes to mind. One day a friend came to me for counsel. She confessed she was struggling with thoughts about things she had done in the past. At this point in her life, she was doing well, cultivating her new marriage and staff position. She couldn't understand why she was dealing with so much shame and guilt after all this time.

I asked her what she had been doing to try and help herself. She explained she'd been getting up early to read her Bible and pray, and she was asking God to give her a word of clarity. Then I took her to the passage in the Bible that speaks to us about being clothed in the righteousness of Christ.

> For he has clothed me with garments of salvation
> and arrayed me in a robe of his righteousness. (Isa.
> 61:10 NIV)

I explained that her enemy, the Devil, wanted her to believe she was still fighting for victory, but this was simply not true. Jesus had already won, so, as a free person, she could now deal with her enemy. I encouraged her to use this scripture each time the enemy came knocking. I told her, "Don't allow your enemy to seduce you. His goal is to trick you into believing you need to know more of the Word to fight him." I encouraged her to use this passage as a *rhema* word to deal with the lie quickly and precisely.

Storehousing

The best way for us to be ready to use these quick, precise words of God is through something I like to call storehousing. When we read the Bible and meditate on the Word of God—whether hearing scripture, singing our theology, or thoughtfully considering God's promises—we fill our pantry. We store up the ingredients we need to live a healthy and vibrant life. We are also preparing for battle.

Then, when our enemy comes—and he will—we will have nothing to fear. We will be prepared and ready. The Spirit of God will reach into our storehouses, the places of our reserves, and grab the ingredients—the precise *rhema* words we need to defeat the enemy.

Consider the words of David in Psalm 119. He knew a thing or two about storehousing the Word of God in his life.

> How can a young person live a clean life?
> By carefully reading the map of your Word.
> I'm single-minded in pursuit of you;

don't let me miss the road signs you've posted.
I've banked your promises in the vault of my heart
so I won't sin myself bankrupt.
Be blessed, GOD;
train me in your ways of wise living.
I'll transfer to my lips
all the counsel that comes from your mouth;
I delight far more in what you tell me about living
than in gathering a pile of riches.
I ponder every morsel of wisdom from you,
I attentively watch how you've done it.
I relish everything you've told me of life,
I won't forget a word of it. (Ps. 119:9–16)

Listen to these phrases: "carefully reading the map of your Word," "I've banked your promises," "I'll transfer to my lips," "I ponder every morsel," "I attentively watch," "I relish everything," and "I won't forget a word of it." Wow, that's a whole lot of storehousing.

God didn't design our warfare to be exhausting and overwhelming. God wants our combat to be quick, swift, and powerful. But it will require us knowing what the Spirit is saying, so we're well equipped when the time comes.

Honestly, you probably won't be able to fight your enemy quickly or precisely if all you have in your scabbard is a Bible verse you received ten years ago. The Spirit of God is ready to give you a fresh and authoritative word, so you can be armed to defeat your enemy today. Don't just take it from me. Jesus used this same strategy when he was on the earth. In the gospel of Luke, we find Jesus in the wilderness. He had been fasting for forty days, and he was hungry. The enemy chose that time to come and tempt him.

> Now Jesus, full of the Holy Spirit, left the Jordan and was led by the Spirit into the wild. For forty wilderness days and nights he was tested by the Devil. He ate nothing during those days, and when the time was up he was hungry. (Luke 4:1–2)

Jesus was truly hungry for food. The enemy knew this, so he came to him and said these words: "Since you're God's Son, command this stone to turn into a loaf of bread" (v. 3).

Our enemy will always try to trap us. He will pick a legitimate need we have and try to convince us to meet it in an illegitimate way. Jesus needed to eat, but he wasn't going to eat simply because the enemy suggested it. He wasn't going to turn those rocks into bread. He knew it was a trap.

This wasn't the first time the enemy tried this. From the beginning, in the garden, the enemy used this exact strategy against Adam and Eve. Did Adam and Eve need to eat? Yes! This was a legitimate need. Were they allowed to eat from every tree in the garden but one? Yes! All the other trees were the legitimate ways to meet their legitimate need. But then the enemy took their freedom to eat and redirected their attention to the one tree God had said they should not touch. Did Adam and Eve end up eating from the Tree of Knowledge of Good and Evil because they were hungry?

I don't think so, but the enemy used a familiar source for meeting their need for food—a tree—and persuaded them it was okay. The enemy didn't offer them something wildly different from what they were accustomed to. He didn't kill an animal in front of them and try to convince them to eat it. He enticed them with an illegitimate source that felt similar to the legitimate sources they'd experienced before, knowing this familiarity would be an advantage.

I'm reminded of a day when I wanted to start being healthier. I had spent the night before making promises to myself, laying out my workout clothes and water bottle and setting my alarm. When I woke up the next morning, I was ready to go. I went to the gym, drank some green juice, and downed my liters of water. But life didn't stop. I had grocery shopping, school pickups, kids' homework, and dinner to make. As the day went on, I found myself wanting to eat, but I didn't have anything ready. I decided not to eat until I could make something healthy. The only problem was, I didn't have any time to make a healthy meal. At the end of the night, feeling utterly famished, I rummaged through the pantry looking for anything to feed this ravished body—and I just ate whatever I could find. It wasn't pretty, and guess what? I went to bed feeling so guilty about what I had eaten and how I had failed at my first attempt to be healthy.

Most of us want to eat the right things, but we are unprepared. We grin and bear it until we can't take it any longer and eat whatever we have in front of us. Then we go to bed feeling full but disappointed and ashamed.

The problem is we are challenging the wrong thing. Our

need and desire to eat is legitimate. But the table where we eat, the place we go for nourishment, is illegitimate.

Let's look at it from one more angle. There's a story in the Bible that makes me want to hit my head against a wall because of the confusion and pure stupidity it puts on display.

> In the spring of the year, when kings normally go out to war, David sent Joab and the Israelite army to fight the Ammonites. They destroyed the Ammonite army and laid siege to the city of Rabbah. However, David stayed behind in Jerusalem.
>
> Late one afternoon, after his midday rest, David got out of bed and was walking on the roof of the palace. As he looked out over the city, he noticed a woman of unusual beauty taking a bath. He sent someone to find out who she was, and he was told, "She is Bathsheba, the daughter of Eliam and the wife of Uriah the Hittite." Then David sent messengers to get her; and when she came to the palace, he slept with her. She had just completed the purification rites after having her menstrual period. Then she returned home. Later, when Bathsheba discovered that she was pregnant, she sent David a message, saying, "I'm pregnant." (2 Sam. 11:1–5 NLT)

Let me paint a picture of what's happening here. David was the type of man that every woman wanted and every man wanted to be. He was handsome, gifted, anointed, and fearless. David was the king of comebacks. He was famous for being a shepherd boy who killed the great Goliath. His success led him to become a nationally recognized warrior and eventually earned him the title of king. His story was one of the greatest stories ever told.

Not only did David wow the nation with his gifts and anointing; he also had a heart of gold. In fact, God called him a man after his own heart. David loved God. He loved him so wholeheartedly that he would worship him without hesitation. At one point he worshiped him until he was only wearing underwear, much to his wife's dismay. But no one could fault David's love and passion for God. He was authentic.

In the middle of this beautiful and powerful story, we find David on a balcony watching someone else's wife bathing. You could almost get whiplash reading this chapter. What was David doing? Why would he, a man of great integrity and honor, do something so dishonorable?

Then David had this woman brought to him and had sex with her. Some commentators would say David raped Bathsheba. Even if David didn't physically rape her, he raped her with his power. She was powerless next to a man of such authority. Eventually she went home, only to send word back that she was pregnant.

God didn't leave this moment alone. He sent a prophet to expose what David had done. He explained that the child would die as a consequence of David's actions. I encourage you to read the rest of the story on your own.

A question I ask when reading this story is: How did David come to a place of such darkness in the first place?

You have to jump back to the beginning of the chapter to find the secret behind this destruction.

The first verse says, "In the spring of the year, when kings normally go out to war." Stop right there. Was David a king? Yes. Was he supposed to be at home or on the battlefield? The battlefield. David's whole life was changed because he made a choice to be at the wrong place at the wrong time. When David should have been at war, he was sitting on a balcony.

David knew he was a king but chose to ignore his true identity and stay home. In that moment, David forgot who he was. I don't mean he forgot about his title; he forgot he was made for the battle. His choice to ignore his true identity left him vulnerable.

David was a child of God, but he wasn't acting like a son. He was acting like an orphan. Orphans believe, "I have needs, and I'm the only one who can meet them." Sons believe, "I have needs, and I have a father who will help me meet them." Both acknowledge their needs, but they run to different sources for help.

I would suggest that David's gaze wasn't wrong; his view was wrong. David's need and desire for a woman was natural. Seeing a naked woman made David want to be with her. It's a normal thing for a healthy man to see a naked woman, regardless of her relationship status, and want to be sexual with her. God made him this way. God wants husbands and wives to have a sexual relationship, and he designed a man to desire his wife—specifically when she is naked!

If David had been on the battlefield, he would have been eating at the king's table. His belly would have been full, and his eyes would have been protected. The moment David chose to forgo the battle was the moment David chose the balcony.

If we are to choose the battle over the balcony, we must remember who we are and trust God to meet our needs. We are God's kids, and he delights in giving us good food to eat. So when we ask him for something and he says no or not now, we don't have to wonder if it's up to us to meet our own needs. We can trust that when God says no, he is trying to protect us; when God says not now, he is trying to prepare us. He never says anything without the best intentions.

It reminds me of Psalm 23:5: "You prepare a table before me in the presence of my enemies" (NIV). In the middle of any situation, God can lay out the best food for us, the best sustenance. In fact, *The Message* translates this verse as: "You serve me a six-course dinner."

So when the Devil came to tempt Jesus back in Luke 4, enticing him to turn the rock into bread, Jesus knew better than to eat the meal the enemy laid out for him.

Jesus answered [the Devil] by quoting Deuteronomy: "It takes more than bread to really live." (Luke 4:4)

Another translation says,

Jesus answered, "It is written: 'Man shall not live on bread alone.'" (NIV)

Jesus said, "It is written" and then quoted Scripture to the enemy. I want to pause right here. Take a moment to see precisely what Jesus did. Jesus didn't say to the enemy, "You'd better stop right there, Satan. Do you remember what happened to me in the previous chapter?"

Let's take a look to refresh our memories.

After all the people were baptized, Jesus was baptized. As he was praying, the sky opened up and the Holy Spirit, like a dove descending, came down on him. And along with the Spirit, a voice: "You are my Son, chosen and marked by my love, pride of my life." (Luke 3:21–22)

Jesus could have said, "Satan, forty days ago I walked into the desert and was greeted by my cousin John. I knew it was time for me to be baptized. When I emerged from the water, the heavens opened, and a loud voice came out of the sky declaring, 'This is my beloved Son, in whom I am well pleased.' Satan, I want you to hear how loved I am. My Father in heaven declared it to all those standing on the shore. Not only that, but the Spirit of God supernaturally came out of the sky in dove form and landed on my shoulder. I am the delight of heaven. Extravagantly loved. Chosen. Adored."

But Jesus didn't do this. He didn't fight his enemy by explaining how loved and affirmed he was by his Father. He didn't say, "I am the most beloved person on the face of the earth. Take that, Satan!" He didn't rehearse, play-by-play, his supernatural encounters with the enemy. Jesus knew the enemy wouldn't be surprised, because Satan knew exactly who Jesus was. He already understood Jesus was utterly adored, the apple of his Father's eye, the chosen Savior.

How does this relate to us? The enemy already knows you are the most loved, adored, chosen, and powerful thing that ever walked this earth. He doesn't need the reminder of how loved and affirmed you are; he needs to be reminded of God's Word. This will silence him every time.

So Jesus, looking at the enemy, used the sword of the Spirit to shut him up. He took a *rhema* word right out of the book of Deuteronomy and, looking straight at the enemy, declared, "It is written."

The enemy tried again.

Then the devil, taking Him up on a high mountain, showed Him all the kingdoms of the world in a moment of time. And the devil said to Him, "All this authority I will give You, and their glory; for this has been delivered to me, and I give it to whomever I wish. Therefore, if You will worship before me, all will be Yours." (Luke 4:5–7 NKJV)

The enemy was hoping Jesus was as power hungry as he was. But Jesus wasn't after power; he was after redemption. So Jesus looked at him and grabbed his *rhema* word again.

And Jesus answered and said to him, "Get behind Me, Satan! For it is written, 'You shall worship the LORD your God, and Him only you shall serve.'" (v 8 NKJV)

Again, the Word of God silenced the enemy.

But the enemy was relentless. He didn't give up. He brought Jesus to Jerusalem, took him to the pinnacle of the temple, and said to him,

If You are the Son of God, throw Yourself down from here. For it is written:

> "He shall give His angels charge over you,
> To keep you," and,
> "In their hands they shall bear you up,
> Lest you dash your foot against a stone." (vv. 9–11 NKJV)

I want you to understand what happened here. The enemy came to Jesus promising to meet an external need—food.

Then he came promising to meet an internal need—glory.

When all that failed, he tried one more thing—Scripture.

Yes, Satan began quoting Scripture to Jesus, hoping he would take the bait. But Jesus knew the only way to fight the Devil was with targeted usage of the Word of God.

> And Jesus answered and said to him, "It has been said, 'You shall not tempt the LORD your God.'" (v. 12 NKJV)

I wonder how many Christians get caught up in the enemy's lies and are manipulated because of misquoted Scripture. Did the enemy quote Scripture correctly? Yes, but just because it's scriptural doesn't mean it's the winning word for the moment.

It's critical that we don't automatically turn to the *logos* to fight the enemy, but we find the quickened, specific *rhema* word given to us by the Spirit. Staying in a daily relationship with the Holy Spirit is vital. Religion can be very dangerous if we end up serving what *once* worked and not what *will* work. We quote the verse God gave us *yesterday*, not the fresh word he desires to give us *today*. When we quote Scripture haphazardly, believing it will keep us safe, we are in danger. Instead, we must continually meditate on the Word of God, building up a vast storehouse of Scripture and maintaining a relationship with the Spirit of God who directs us on how to use it. He wants to speak to us. Protect us. Lay a weapon in our hands to defeat the enemy at the right moment.

As I studied this passage of Scripture, I pictured Jesus standing in the desert, weak, frail, and hungry. Each time the enemy came to hurt him, Jesus would reach his hand behind him, and the Holy Spirit would place a weapon in his hand. Jesus would then use it against his enemy, and the enemy would flee. Each time, three times, every time, Jesus used a specific word.

Like Jesus, each time we face a lie, we have the same weapon available to us. All we need to do is listen to the Holy Spirit. When he says, "Reach your hand behind you; I'm about to give you what you need to defeat your enemy," you'll be ready!

Rhema in the Everyday

In our last chapter, I told you about the pastor who spoke discouraging words to me in Arizona. I confessed that his words continued to have power over me throughout the years. I would get up to speak, and all I would hear was, *They don't want what you have. You're too young, too ignorant, too aggressive.* Then one day I came across this scripture:

> Get the word out. Teach all these things. And don't let anyone put you down because you're young. Teach believers with your life: by word, by demeanor, by love, by faith, by integrity. Stay at your post reading Scripture, giving counsel, teaching. And that special gift of ministry you were given when the leaders of the church laid hands on you and prayed—keep that dusted off and in use. (1 Tim. 4:11–14)

The Holy Spirit immediately quickened me. He said, "This is the word for your season." I knew God had placed this weapon in my hand, and I was going to use it.

The next time I got up to speak, all the same anxiety and fear flooded my heart and mind. Before, I would try to worship the fear away or try to ignore it, treating it like a fly that wouldn't leave me alone. But this time was different. I wasn't trying to brush it away. I wasn't trying to drown it out with my praise. I looked the lie in the face and said, "Enemy! I'm not going to let you look down on me anymore. I'm going to set an example with my life, my words, my demeanor, my love, my faith, and my integrity. I am resisting you! You must flee, or you're going to come under my authority in Christ."

Almost instantaneously, I felt a complete breakthrough. The restraints on my heart were released, and I was finally free. Later on, each time that same old stupid lie would rear its dirty head, I would say the same scripture to the enemy. I wielded it like a sword in my hand. My *rhema* word. I was stabbing the enemy, thrusting his lie through with the truth.

Another time the Holy Spirit gave me a *rhema* word was when I was embarrassed about some of my personal decisions. I asked God to forgive me for my mistakes, but each time I got up to preach, the enemy would say to me, *You are such a hypocrite. You're two-faced and double-minded. If people knew what you did, they would never listen to you.* I went to work looking for my sword of the Spirit.

The Holy Spirit took me to this scripture:

> I delight greatly in the LORD;
> my soul rejoices in my God.
> For he has clothed me with garments of salvation
> and arrayed me in a robe of his righteousness,
> as a bridegroom adorns his head like a priest,
> and as a bride adorns herself with her jewels. (Isa.
>   61:10 NIV)

Right then and there, I knew I was clothed in the righteousness of Christ. I wasn't clothed in my shame anymore. The Holy Spirit continued to teach me, showing me Galatians 2:19–21:

> What actually took place is this: I tried keeping rules and working my head off to please God, and it didn't work. So I quit being a "law man" so that I could be God's man. Christ's life showed me how, and enabled me to

do it. I identified myself completely with him. Indeed, I have been crucified with Christ. My ego is no longer central. It is no longer important that I appear righteous before you or have your good opinion, and I am no longer driven to impress God. Christ lives in me. The life you see me living is not "mine," but it is lived by faith in the Son of God, who loved me and gave himself for me. I am not going to go back on that. Is it not clear to you that to go back to that old rule-keeping, peer-pleasing religion would be an abandonment of everything personal and free in my relationship with God? I refuse to do that, to repudiate God's grace. If a living relationship with God could come by rule-keeping, then Christ died unnecessarily.

When the enemy came to torment and silence me, I would tell him, "I'm in right standing with Christ. I'm a new creation. It is no longer important that I appear righteous before you or have your good opinion, and I am no longer driven to impress God. Christ lives in me. Greater is he who lives in me than he who lives in the world. You know what, Devil? As far as the east is from the west, that's how far Christ has removed my guilt from me. Enemy, if you want to hang out here and accuse me, I might just enclose you with the righteousness of Christ too."

After all these years, God has faithfully given me a *rhema* word for every season. I'm convinced he will do the same for you. My *rhema* word doesn't have to mean anything to you, but it means the world to me. Sometimes I've received it through a text message from a friend. Other times it's been a scripture in a song or a sermon I've heard. Usually it has come to me as I've been in my *logos*, storehousing my weapons.

The Bible says in 2 Corinthians,

> The world is unprincipled. It's dog-eat-dog out there! The world doesn't fight fair. But we don't live or fight our battles that way—never have and never will. The tools of our trade aren't for marketing or manipulation, but they are for demolishing that entire massively corrupt culture. We use our powerful God-tools for smashing warped philosophies, tearing down barriers erected against the truth of God, fitting every loose thought and emotion and impulse into the structure of life shaped by Christ. Our tools are ready at hand for clearing the ground of every obstruction and building lives of obedience into maturity. (10:3–6)

The word *warfare* is taken from the word *stratos*, and the word *stratos* is the root of the word *strategy*. The scriptures are telling us that we must have God's strategy in order to win our battles.

Just as any army plans its line of attack before a battle begins, the Devil plans a line of attack, decides which methods he will use, and chooses the best approach to take out his targets. He cautiously charts his assault.

But the word *stratos* doesn't just describe the Devil's strategies. It also suggests that if we listen to the Holy Spirit, he will give us a strategy that is superior to any schemes of the Devil. The Devil is not the only one with a strategy. The Holy Spirit holds the key to every victory, and he wants to provide us with a divinely inspired strategy that will render null and void the works of the Devil—every time!

EMPOWERMENT POINTS

- Our enemy is defeated, but we still need to know how to deal with him.
- When we read the Bible and meditate on the Word of God—whether hearing scripture, singing our theology, or thoughtfully considering God's promises—we fill our pantry. We store up the ingredients we need to live a healthy and vibrant life.
- When our enemy comes—and he will—we will have nothing to fear. We will be prepared and ready. The Spirit of God will reach into our storehouses, the places of our reserves, and grab the ingredients—the precise *rhema* words we need to defeat the enemy.
- The Spirit of God is ready to give you a fresh and authoritative word, so you can be armed to defeat your enemy today.
- Our enemy will always try to trap us. He will pick a legitimate need we have and try to convince us to meet it in an illegitimate way.

Chapter 9

Everyday Battles,
Everyday Wins

The phone rang. I was home alone with my four young sons and was starting to fall apart in my new mom-of-four season. It had been a crazy year. Actually, it had been the craziest five years of my life. We'd had four sons in five years of marriage, which included four pregnancies, four C-sections, and four hospital stays. The last birth in particular had been a doozy. Beckham came into the world healthy at thirty-seven weeks, but his oxygen levels were low and he was immediately admitted to the NICU. Thus began our daily trips to the hospital.

I would come home to my three little bears to snuggle

and connect, only to return to the hospital to feed my infant son. Meanwhile I was still recovering from my fourth C-section, which was almost more than I could physically bear. When we finally took Beckham home, I was hopeful that things would calm down and I would get to settle into our new life. But on a quick trip to the store, I noticed red bumps on my one-and-a-half-year-old Grayson's mouth that were concerning. When you have a preemie at home, you don't mess around, so I loaded up our boys and took them to the Urgent Care Center. We left with a diagnosis of hand, foot, and mouth disease for the older three kids and a quarantine for ten days. It had been one thing after another, but I was keeping my head above water, believing this was only a season.

Before long the phone rang, and I heard my husband on the other end: "Honey, I have some really hard news. Our church is letting us go. They can't find the finances to keep us on staff any longer. Everyone is incredibly sad. It's been a very hard decision, but they need to do it at this time. They waited as long as they could, but there's no way around it. I'm so sorry, sweetheart."

Holding the phone, I didn't say a word. I was in shock. I quickly told him I needed to go and couldn't talk right then. Hanging up, I thought I might lose my mind at that very moment. But I knew better than to lose it in front of our boys. I ran into our bedroom, closed the door behind me, face-planted on our bed, and sobbed uncontrollably. I threw a full-blown adult tantrum. This news was almost more than I could bear. My phone flooded with calls from my concerned family, but I quickly denied them. What could I say? I could barely think, let alone speak.

I began a conversation with God. I said, "God, I don't understand you. I have given you my whole life. I have rarely said no to you. Anything you've asked of me I have done wholeheartedly and with all my strength. Now, at the end of all of this, you take the very thing I need. I've been on staff at this church for over fifteen years. I was here in the beginning, and I planned on being here till the end." I was letting God have it. I continued, "What do you expect me to do? It's not as though I can give the baby back. I can't nurse my entire family to feed them." Sarcasm. "What do you expect me to do? What do you want me to do?" (Insert sob.)

Through my tears, I heard the Holy Spirit say to me, "I want you to make chicken." That was all he said.

I thought maybe I had misunderstood him. Frustrated, I said, "You want me to what? Make chicken? Why don't you make chicken yourself?!" I grinned, thinking about the fact that God had made chicken quite literally.

He said, "I want you to get up, clean up the house and the boys, and prepare for Ben to come home."

As I lay there, my other three sons managed to break into the room and were now jumping on the bed and climbing all over me. "Mommy, are you sad?" "Mommy, what's wrong?"

I whispered to God, "Well, I have nothing else to do other than what you said. I'm going to make chicken." I took the kids into the bathroom, gave them a warm bath, and put them in their favorite jammies. Cleaning up our little house,

I managed to light a few candles, pop on some Diana Krall music, and set the table. I was ready.

As Ben walked in the door, his face was melancholy. Hesitant to say anything, he slowly asked, "Do you want to talk?"

I looked at him, took a deep breath, and said, "No, can we eat dinner first?"

He was confused. I think most married men reading this may understand. We wives spend years training our husbands never to take us at our first response to the question, "Do you want to talk?" The question needs asking at least two times—that is, if you really care. These are girl rules. We're not being manipulative; it's just part of the pursuit. We want to know that you're listening and you care. If we feel safe, we will open our hearts.

Ben asked again, "Are you sure? Don't you want to talk?"

This time, with a little more confidence, I said, "No, I would like to eat dinner. We can put the boys to bed and then talk." I honestly think he looked a little relieved.

We ate our dinner. I want you to know I make one of the best chicken dinners you'll ever eat, but it wasn't the secret to nurturing the peace that lingered in our home that night. The secret to peace is obeying the Prince of Peace. That night, the act of standing in a spiritual place even in the face of adversity grounded me. The Holy Spirit was right. Chicken dinner was exactly what we needed to be eating.

Please understand the phone did not ring that night while we were eating dinner, offering us new dream jobs. Nope. In fact, we waited weeks before we knew what we were going to do next. But the breakthrough came the moment I decided to get up and make chicken. After that moment, I never lost hope again. The powerful expression of the Holy Spirit caring about the smallest details and our regular needs empowered us in our everyday. His consideration for something as simple as what we were going to eat that night grounded me in his love for us. We were going to be okay, even if it cost us a little.

Sometimes the Holy Spirit gives us a direction that seems opposite of how we would typically respond to a difficult situation. Honestly, I wanted to give up that night, pack up my bags and my babies, and run home to my parents. And you know what? They would've gladly received us, fed us a warm meal, and tucked the boys into cozy beds. But running home wouldn't have taught me how God wants me to win in my everyday battles.

Move Out to Move In

The Holy Spirit will always invite us to step into our miracle. I'm reminded of the story in the Bible about a man who was sick for an extremely long time. Let's read it together:

> Soon another Feast came around and Jesus was back in Jerusalem. Near the Sheep Gate in Jerusalem there was a pool, in Hebrew called *Bethesda*, with five alcoves. Hundreds of sick people—blind, crippled, paralyzed—were in these alcoves. One man had been an invalid there

for thirty-eight years. When Jesus saw him stretched out by the pool and knew how long he had been there, he said, "Do you want to get well?" (John 5:1–6)

Jesus walked on the scene and knew what was taking place. News of this pool had spread near and far in their community, so many had gathered in hopes of receiving their miracle. Jesus saw a man who had been sick almost his entire life. And now the man was sitting at the pond with everyone else, hoping to be healed.

Then Jesus walked up to him and asked, "Do you want to get well?"

Can you even imagine? This man was obviously very ill, and Jesus had the nerve to ask if he would like to get well. Why would Jesus ask such a question? He wasn't confused. When Jesus asked a question, it was always because the answer held the miracle. He never wasted words.

Jesus asked this man, "Do you want to get well?" And the man responded. His answer revealed what had kept him ill.

The sick man said, "Sir, when the water is stirred, I don't have anybody to put me in the pool. By the time I get there, somebody else is already in" (v. 7).

Two specific things this man communicated show us the state of his heart. The first thing he mentioned was having no one to put him in the pool.

If I were preaching this to you in person, I would ask you to underline the phrase, "I don't have anybody." This sentence reveals his perceived reality. After thirty-eight years, he could not find one person to help him into the pool? I don't buy it. At this point, all he needed was to lie on the edge of the pool and ask a friend to give him a swift kick. Ha! A simple definition for *self-pity* is self-absorbed unhappiness over one's own troubles. Self-pity has the interesting effect of leaving us feeling isolated and alone. It blocks us of hope, connection, and relationship. This man personified self-pity.

Many of us are just like this man. We sit in places of sickness, pain, isolation, and self-pity because it's easier to live in defeat than it is to admit we've allowed ourselves to get to this place. It's much easier to look at someone who has more than we do and believe his or her journey has been easier and more comfortable. We might even be right, but that doesn't negate the facts of where we are now. Everyone must choose to show up for a miracle. No one can show up for us.

The next thing this man revealed to us is at the end of his sentence. He said, "By the time I get there, somebody else is already in."

You're telling me that after thirty-eight years of sickness and multiple opportunities to get well by touching the water, he couldn't get there fast enough? If it were me, I would tell my buddy next to me, "When you see the water move, could you give me a little shove?" Come on!

It wasn't his opportunity to get well that was distracting him; it was everyone else's. He was living in comparison, and comparison will always render us powerless.

I remember when the Holy Spirit revealed the truth about comparison to me. He said, "Comparison is the enemy's way of convincing you that God cheated you." One of the enemy's greatest weapons is convincing you to live in comparison. If we keep looking at someone else, we will never see God at work in our lives.

So when Jesus asked the man if he wanted to get well, he was asking him if he wanted his power back. He meant, "Are you ready to stop wallowing in defeat and being distracted by comparison? Are you ready to be powerful? Are you ready to be whole? Are you willing to show up like a grown-up?" This man had used every excuse in the book, but his excuses weren't healing him. He blamed everyone else but never took personal responsibility.

He must have realized this, because in the next moment we see an immediate change.

Jesus said, "Get up, take your bedroll, start walking." The man was healed on the spot. He picked up his bedroll and walked off. (v. 8–9)

Jesus offered this man a moment to be powerful. It's interesting that Jesus didn't pick the man up, roll up his bedroll, and help him walk. No, Jesus looked at him and invited him to get up, roll up his bed, and get moving himself. The man did exactly that and was instantly healed. In the same way, Jesus will invite us into a moment where we can respond to him in faith, or we can stay where we are in unbelief.

Often, we have to move out in order to go in. We have to move out of fear to walk into courage. We have to move out of shame to walk into purity. We have to move out of anxiety and worry to walk into peace and rest. Jesus will not do it for us, but he will invite us into it. He made a way for us to have our miracle.

Let's look at another man in the Bible who modeled the right mentality of proactively stepping into God's victory:

> As Jesus went into Capernaum, a centurion came up to Him, begging Him [for help], and saying, "Lord, my servant is lying at home paralyzed, with intense and terrible, tormenting pain." Jesus said to him, "I will come and heal him." But the centurion replied to Him, "Lord, I am not worthy to have You come under my roof, but only say the word, and my servant will be healed. For I also am a man subject to authority [of a higher rank], with soldiers subject to me; and I say to one, 'Go!' and he goes, and to another, 'Come!' and he comes, and to my slave, 'Do this!' and he does it." When Jesus heard this, He was amazed and said to those who were following Him, "I tell you truthfully, I have not found such great faith [as this] with anyone in Israel." (Matt. 8:5–10 AMP)

Unlike the sick man who lay next to the pool, the centurion was used to knowing what he was responsible for and doing just that to make things happen. He was used to his voice moving men. He was used to taking responsibility. He was used to doing his part so others could do theirs.

How did this help him get the miracle he needed?

He couldn't solve the problem himself, but he did what he could. He couldn't heal the servant, but he could go to someone who might be willing to do it for him. He didn't sit on his own, saying, "Poor me. Why has this happened to me? What am I going to do now? Life is so hard." He may have had those thoughts initially, but eventually, he went out to do something about it. His mentality was, "I can't do everything, but I can do something."

Irresponsible people will always believe their circumstances define them. They find it impossible to see past their own limitations. They are obsessed with believing it's someone else's job to show up for things to really change. They need someone else to participate in order for them to be hopeful or happy. They see themselves as victims.

Responsible people will look for more options. They believe they have a part to play and are willing to do their portion. They understand everyone has a responsibility to show up if everything is going to work. The centurion showed up like a spiritual grown-up. He was ready to do his part, even if his task was to just believe and ask Jesus to help. In fact, he was so confident that if he played his role well and Jesus played his, everything would eventually work out—and it did: "Then Jesus said to the centurion, 'Go; it will be done for you as you have believed.' And the servant was restored to health at that very hour" (v. 13 AMP).

EMPOWERMENT POINTS

- The secret to peace is obeying the Prince of Peace.

- The powerful expression of the Holy Spirit caring about the smallest details and our regular needs empowers us in our everyday lives.
- The Holy Spirit will always invite us to step into our miracle.
- When Jesus asked a question, it was always because the answer held the miracle.
- Comparison is the enemy's way of convincing you that God cheated you.
- Jesus will invite us into a moment where we can respond to him in faith, or we can stay where we are in unbelief.
- I can't do everything, but I can do something.

Chapter 10

Shake the Dust

*I*t was my first time visiting China, and I was extremely excited. I had spent months preparing for this international experience. At the time, we did not have iPhones, iPads, or digital cameras, so we had to capture our journey on a simple Kodak with a few rolls of film. I was armed and ready to capture every moment of this surreal trip.

Those two weeks of travel included some of the best experiences of my life. Landing on the island of Hong Kong, we consumed every morsel of the culture: boat trips, temple ruins, marketplaces, and historical landmarks. And that was just the beginning. We also spent a few days in Chengdu and then went on to Tibet. It was the journey of a lifetime.

When I arrived home, I hurried to have the film developed,

desperately wanting to relive this epic voyage. The photographs would help convey the full experience to my loved ones. Having my film developed was a three-day process, so at the end of the week, I trekked back to pick up my twelve packs of photos. I even paid extra to have them duplicated, so I could give them to other teammates.

Running into the drugstore, I grabbed my photos and then settled in my car to privately enjoy the moment. Tearing open the first envelope, I smiled to myself. But then I stopped in my tracks. Something was wrong. Terribly wrong. A large white dot marred the left-hand corner of every photo. I quickly thumbed through the whole set, hoping my eyes were deceiving me. Disappointed, I threw them in the passenger seat and tore open the next envelope. The same. Each set, all twelve rolls of the film, were ruined. A speck of dust on my lens had hindered the production of clear pictures, and without a digital display, I'd had no way to see it at the time. Only after developing the film did I notice the flaw on each picture. The horror was more than I could bear. I sat there stunned, sick to my stomach, realizing I could not get back what I had lost. The blemish on my lens had ruined these once-in-a-lifetime photographs.

Dust Is a Distraction

Jesus pointed out another kind of dust that similarly affects what we see, distracting each of us from a healthy perspective on our lives. Let's follow the story starting in Matthew 10:

Jesus summoned His twelve disciples and gave them authority and power over unclean spirits, to cast them out, and to heal every kind of disease and every kind of sickness. (v. 1 AMP)

What a truly powerful moment. It's hard to fully grasp what was happening here, so let me take a moment to explain it. Jesus was preparing his disciples for his eventual departure from earth. He knew he was going to die, be resurrected in three days, ascend into heaven, and leave the planet altogether. So he was equipping his disciples to continue his work after his ascension. The mood would have been somber and intentional. For example, imagine a young mother being diagnosed with a terminal illness and her family gathering to make plans. She would know she only had a short season, maybe three years, to communicate her heart to her family. Her words would be weighty, her language intentional. She would understand the significance of the moment and the legacy of her words.

Jesus, in the same way, was communicating his commissioning words. He was impassioned to give his disciples, his young spiritual family, words to live out—ideas that would keep them healthy and safe when he was no longer there. Jesus called them, anointed them, and instructed them. He continued,

Whatever city or village you enter, ask who in it is worthy [who welcomes you and your message], and stay at his house until you leave [that city]. As you go into the house, give it your greeting [that is, "Peace be to this house"]. If [the family living in] the house is worthy [welcoming you and your message], give it your [blessing of] peace [that is, a blessing of well-being and prosperity, the favor of God]. But if it is not worthy, take back your blessing of peace. Whoever does not welcome you, nor listen to your message, as you leave that house or city, shake the dust [of it] off your feet [in contempt, breaking all ties]." (vv. 11–14 AMP)

Jesus was preparing his disciples for conflict when he said, "If any place will not welcome you or listen to you, leave that place and shake off the dust off your feet as a testimony against them" (Mark 6:11 NIV).

Why would Jesus say, "Shake off the dust"? Historically when Jews returned to Israel from pagan lands, they would shake the "Gentile dirt" off their feet and move on, declaring it unworthy of the land of God's people.

Jesus used an illustration his disciples would understand, but he gave it new meaning. His words were meant to comfort them. He encouraged them by explaining that if rejection happened to Jesus, then it would happen to them as well.

The disciple John captured what Jesus was saying in his account:

If you find the godless world is hating you, remember it got its start hating me. If you lived on the world's terms, the world would love you as one of its own. But since I picked you to live on God's terms and no longer on the world's terms, the world is going to hate you. (John 15:18–19)

"The world is going to hate you." In other words, the dust we must shake off our feet is *offense*. This includes any unresolved issues or ugly residues of conflict. Jesus encouraged his young leaders to watch out for this dust in their lives. It's not just personal; it's spiritual.

Trigger for the Trap

So why is it so important to look for offense? Why is offense so dangerous when it comes to our spiritual lives?

First, we need to understand that the Bible doesn't say *if* offenses should come; it says *when*. Jesus even said it was impossible for offenses *not* to come.

> Then He said to the disciples, "It is impossible that no offenses should come, but woe to him through whom they do come!" (Luke 17:1 NKJV)

Jesus wasn't picking out a few people and talking to them about what to do in a rare instance of offense. No, he was saying, "Look, guys, it's coming, and I want to give you a strategy. Do not let offenses overwhelm you." I love how the Amplified Bible says it so directly:

> Jesus said to His disciples, "Stumbling blocks [temptations and traps set to lure one to sin] are sure to come, but woe (judgment is coming) to him through whom they come!"

This version gives us a portion of the Greek we would otherwise miss in another version: "Stumbling blocks [temptations and traps set to lure one to sin]." An offense means *the trigger of the trap*.

Years ago we had a possum problem. Yes, you read that right. During my middle school years in Los Angeles, we lived in the small town of Sierra Madre, which is nestled right near the mountains of Pasadena. Sierra Madre is a beautiful place to live, but it also attracted wild animals. If you've ever seen a possum, you know these creatures look like giant, hideous rats. You wouldn't want to catch one on your own.

When we discovered we had this problem, we immediately called Animal Control to help us. They brought two traps to capture the possums and take them away. The traps were metal cages with food placed inside, and when a possum walked into the trap, the little trigger was unlatched and the door slammed shut, closing the animal inside. Week after week they found these furry little beasts. We were all relieved and a little traumatized to see what had been roaming around our backyard.

Those traps would have been nothing without the triggers that made the doors slam shut, and that's exactly what offense does when we let it take hold in our lives. I love how clear the Bible is about this. It doesn't pull any punches. The original Greek word used in the verse is *skándalon*, which is defined as the trigger of a trap. The word choice implies that offense is the trigger to the trap; it can lead us toward a life of animosity, bitterness, and unforgiveness.

An offense is treacherous to our spiritual lives. It gives

our enemy access to our hearts, to the deepest parts of our souls. The apostle Paul warned us in Ephesians, "Do not give the devil an opportunity [to lead you into sin by holding a grudge, or nurturing anger, or harboring resentment, or cultivating bitterness]" (4:27 AMP). We end up building offended places in our minds, and conflicts can often create cracks or entry points for the enemy. Once the wall is constructed, it will eventually separate us from the people we need and love the most.

Another meaning in Greek for the word *offense* relates to trespassing. When we are offended and allow ourselves to make judgments about what belongs to others—judging their feelings, attitudes, or choices—we end up trespassing. We are called to influence others but not to parent them. We are not to take up what is not ours. When we do, it becomes another way our enemy tries to bring judgment on us. He knows the Bible says, "In the same way you judge others, you will be judged" (Matt. 7:2 NIV). If the enemy can convince you to judge others, you will be trapped in judgment as well.

Instead, we need to shake off the offense that wants to adhere itself to us, impeding movement, suffocating our hearts, leaving us feeling hopeless. It's like the time the apostle Paul was shipwrecked on an island. He had been trying to evangelize but with no success. Washing up onto the shore, he began to make a fire. Let's jump right into the story.

> But when Paul had gathered a bundle of sticks and laid
> them on the fire, a viper crawled out because of the heat

and fastened itself on his hand. When the natives saw the creature hanging from his hand, they began saying to one another, "Undoubtedly this man is a murderer, and though he has been saved from the sea, Justice [the avenging goddess] has not permitted him to live." Then Paul [simply] shook the creature off into the fire and suffered no ill effects. But they stood watching and expecting him to swell up or suddenly drop dead. But after they had waited a long time and had seen nothing unusual happen to him, they changed their minds. (Acts 28:3–6 AMP)

Paul's ability to shake off that which tried to adhere itself to him was a testimony to everyone watching. Our lives should be lived out in the same way. When others see us not allowing offenses to take root in our hearts or minds but fighting off this spirit, they will see God at work in us.

What are some common offenses? Let's make a list so we can watch out for them.

- When people you thought would stay by your side leave you
- When money you thought would come never comes
- When caring for a broken person in your life leaves you overwhelmed and exhausted
- When disappointment is placed on you by others
- When you are heartbroken
- When you suffer loss

- When you are rejected
- When ministry opportunities you hoped for don't materialize
- When God doesn't come through for you the way you thought he would

Honestly, it doesn't matter if we have a legitimate reason for offense or if we're nursing a self-inflicted wound. It comes down to how we want to live. If we really want to be free—living a healthy and whole spiritual life, free from the Devil's drama—then we have to remove offense from our lives, being vigilant to keep offense as far away from our hearts as possible.

When we hold on to offense, we hold on to a grudge, to the scratch on our lens. The flaw keeps us from seeing our lives clearly. It keeps us from looking back and enjoying the journey. The hard truth is, not every person or place is going to welcome you in, and sometimes it will be better to leave, shake the dust off, and keep going. Let's not give the enemy an opportunity to make cracks in our lives. Shake off the dust!

EMPOWERMENT POINTS

- The Bible doesn't say *if* offenses should come; it says *when*. Jesus even said it was impossible for offenses *not* to come.

- Offense is the trigger to the trap; it can lead us toward a life of animosity, bitterness, and unforgiveness.
- When others see us not allowing offenses to take root in our hearts or minds but fighting off this spirit, they will see God at work in us.
- When we hold on to offense, we hold on to a grudge, to the scratch on our lens. The flaw keeps us from seeing our lives clearly.

Chapter 11

Uncomplicating Your Spiritual Battle

I pulled the boys close. "Now, boys, I have some exciting news. Your dad and I want to take you to Disneyland in a few short weeks. Isn't that exciting?" My news was greeted with the joy I had anticipated. The boys were thrilled. I went on: "Now, if you boys would like to earn some money to take with you as spending money, I have an idea. I'll make a list of chores, and with each task you complete, I'll give you a dollar."

Every parent understands it's best to use these types of opportunities as leverage. I figured they could tackle a few things that needed to be done and build some character at the same time. I could give them some money to spend and simultaneously limit their spending money. It was a win-win!

Our firstborn, Judah David, was all over it. His eyes got enormous as I explained to him the potential. His head nodded. He had a determined look on his face; he was ready. Through all my reading about firstborns, I've learned they usually like to take the opportunity to lead, specifically if there is a reward. They love parameters, rules, and expectations. Maybe it's because they've been on the earth a little longer and understand how Mom and Dad operate.

Hudson Samuel, our second born, is a classic middle child. He's always moving, climbing anything that can be climbed, including his parents. As I expressed my invitation, Hudson barely looked at me. Honestly, he couldn't have cared less. I knew he understood what I was suggesting; he just didn't want any part of it.

After our talk, Judah ran off to begin the chores almost immediately. Hudson followed but only to watch Judah. A little while later I found both boys cleaning windows. I asked, "Are you boys both working to earn your money?"

Judah exclaimed, "Oh, no. I'm working, and Hudson's helping me."

Apparently Judah had figured out a way to utilize his younger brother's energy to his benefit—another firstborn tendency.

As the weeks went on, checklists were crossed off, and I handed out dollar bills. Judah had earned a total of fourteen dollars, and Hudson had made a total of zero. But none of that mattered as we climbed into our SUV with three car seats, luggage shoved into every crack and crevice, and two exhausted parents ready to make the eight-hour drive.

Judah suggested I purchase a wallet for him a week prior so he could hold his money better. I didn't mind; I love being able to help him celebrate his success.

On our way out of town, I remembered Grandma had given Hudson a card. We were calling our trip Hudson's birthday trip. Honestly, we had planned on going anyway, but when you have a lot of kids, you make different events birthday events. It's the ugly truth about parenting large families. Hudson didn't get any gifts that year, other than this trip to Disneyland and a card from his grandparents.

We passed the card back to him in the third row. He was sitting in the only seat available with luggage surrounding him. Judah sat in the second row, wedged between the two car seats holding his younger brothers Grayson and Beckham.

When Hudson opened the card, he began to shout. He lifted up the card in one hand and the gift in the other—a twenty-dollar bill! Grandma and Grandpa had sent Hudson twenty dollars to celebrate his birthday in Disneyland. When we saw Hudson holding his twenty-dollar gift, we began to hoop and holler. It was like *The Price Is Right* in the middle of our SUV. "Hudson, that's so awesome, son! Look what you just got for your birthday! A twenty-dollar bill. Happy birthday, Hudson!" We knew this was Hudson's birthday moment, so we milked it.

All of a sudden, in the midst of our celebration, I thought

about Judah. I looked down to check on him, and our eyes met at the same time. I could see he was in distress. His big brown eyes were filled halfway with huge tears; he was barely keeping it together.

At that moment I exclaimed, "Oh, Judah, does that make you sad?" My words broke his emotional dam. Judah let out a huge scream, and now tears streamed down his face. Judah had worked so hard for his fourteen dollars, and now Hudson instantly had twenty dollars. As a firstborn child, it was almost more than he could bear.

I went into Mom Mode. Like most parents I was empathetic. "Oh, Judah!" I said. "I'm so sorry. I know that must be so tough. Please remember this is Hudson's birthday, and this is his only gift. I know it's hard, but can we celebrate Hudson? We would do the same thing for you."

Judah was not buying it. The more I tried to console him, the more he lost it.

So, I went into Coach Mode. "You know, son, sometimes you just gotta push through it. Life isn't fair, so you'd better stop waiting for it to be fair. You'll have to suck it up and be okay. You can do this, Judah!"

Still no resolve.

Using all my tools and techniques to calm Judah down, I found my last reserve, a place most parents don't like to access when they're desperate: Prison Guard Mode. "Judah, if you don't calm down, I'm going to turn this car around. We will just go home. You don't have to go to Disneyland. We'll leave you with Grandma and Grandpa, and take your little brothers to Disneyland."

Before you judge, most of us know parenting brings out the best and the worst in us. Ben looked at me as if to say, *I'm sorry, what? We are not turning this car around. It took me three hours to pack it correctly so that we could all fit.*

Then I leaned over and said something to Judah. When I said it, the Holy Spirit whispered to me, *What you just said to Judah is exactly what I've been saying to you!* I was leaning over the passenger seat, looking at Judah with confidence, saying, "Judah, you are not going to go without! Judah, you are going to Disneyland. All of your needs are going to be well taken care of. You are not going to go without. Trust me." At that moment the Holy Spirit showed me a picture of what our spiritual lives resemble.

Most of our spiritual lives and spiritual battles look like fourteen-dollar days. If we work hard and remain diligent, we reap a reward. God will be faithful to us, but we still have to do our part. We have to take every thought captive. We have to surrender our will—yes, even the strong-willed ones—at the feet of Jesus, letting God have the final vote. We have to trust God when we can't see where we are going. We have to call the enemy out consistently on what he's doing and keep him under our feet.

But every once in a while, God in his miraculous power will give us a twenty-dollar moment. We'll receive an immediate supernatural healing. We'll experience a breakthrough from an addiction that never returns. The money will come in the mail, even though we had no way of earning it. God will give us a twenty-dollar moment when we least expect it and have no way of earning it. A twenty-dollar miracle.

Then we will witness someone else around us having a twenty-dollar moment. We'll see someone else get married before we do. Or a friend will be offered a position we are more qualified to hold. Or an opportunity we prayed for will be dropped right in the lap of someone else. We may be going through our fourteen-dollar days wondering what we're doing wrong. It's not that we're not receiving any compensation; our typical days just aren't as flashy and miraculous as someone else's.

Realizing that it's not our job to judge if somebody deserves his or her twenty-dollar moment is critical to our satisfaction. It's our responsibility to celebrate and stay diligent in our fourteen-dollar days. Judah was happy to receive his money. He worked hard, but not hard enough to earn all of that money. Mommy and Daddy were still generous. God is the same with us. We don't deserve as much as he is willing and wants to give. He's that good. We only get distracted or feel cheated when we look at what others have received. Don't do it. Comparison will drain you of your strength and resolve.

Your spiritual warfare might look like a fourteen-dollar day, but that doesn't mean it's not working. You may have to say no to that addiction every single day. You may be calling the enemy out every single time, needing to stay on alert. Every victory you've experienced can be traced to a moment of a whole lot of hustle and a whole lot of heart. But your effort doesn't diminish in value, and everyday battles are worthy and courageous. Besides, your twenty-dollar moment may be just around the corner.

Secrets to Overcoming the Struggle

As we all continue faithfully in our fourteen-dollar days, allow me to offer up some advice that I hope will keep you going. Here are some of the best-kept secrets to my own success in winning everyday battles.

When I used to think about spiritual warfare, I imagined it involved some grandiose prayer meeting, conquering the gates of hell, a killer worship team, and a fiery pastor. And it can include those things, but in most cases the fight is simply doing what God has put right in front of us—living as Christ has called each of us to live.

I'm convinced spiritual things look as practical as they do supernatural. There isn't a sacred and secular line in God's eyes. Everything we do is sacred to God. This is how Paul encourages us in Colossians: "Whatever you do, work at it with all your heart, as working for the Lord, not for human masters" (3:23 NIV).

Paul reminds us that God isn't as concerned with what we do as he is with how we do it. God is present in the details, in the everyday motions. God doesn't want us to waste time chasing after some mysterious, elusive will. He wants us to embody him in our everyday, between-the-washer-and-the-dryer lives.

The Bible says, "Go into all the world," and for me, most of the time, that means walking into my living room. My life consists of sharing Jesus in a practical way to my congregation of four: my sons. What I do in my little home holds just as much value as what I do out in the world. God sees it as the same thing. So let's look together at some practical steps we can take in our daily lives in order to win the spiritual battles happening all around us.

Bedtimes and Sleep Schedules

The Bible says our enemy roams around like a roaring lion seeking whom he may devour.

> Be sober [well balanced and self-disciplined], be alert and cautious at all times. That enemy of yours, the devil, prowls around like a roaring lion [fiercely hungry], seeking someone to devour. (1 Peter 5:8 AMP)

If you study lions, you'll learn something interesting. Lions like to hunt at night and early in the morning. Our enemy does the same thing. Interestingly enough, most of my struggles and internal battles have been at night. Why is this? Our enemy knows when we are tired, and sleep deprivation makes it hard for us to stay at ease under stress. Our brains function at limited efficiency. Tiredness magnifies stress and decreases problem-solving ability. It leaves us susceptible to the enemy's attacks.

Another reason our enemy attacks us at night is he knows our community isn't always available in the evening. He lures us when we are isolated and the most vulnerable. We are most powerful when we are around our community, our pack, our tribe. So it makes sense that many of our battles will take place when we're not in the safety of that community.

Research has found that sleep not only increases our

ability to be more efficient, but also rids the brain of toxins. It's the only way for the brain to cleanse itself. Science continues to find more and more benefits to the power of sleep. It is vital to being healthy: mentally, physically, emotionally, and spiritually.

When I survey my success and failures, I see clearly that nighttime isn't when I make the best decisions. I know I'm not alone in this. Many of us find ourselves having Facebook meltdowns, watching things we wish we hadn't, and doing activities that leave us with the morning-after feeling—all because we didn't go to bed and put ourselves to sleep when we should have.

When I discovered this, the first thing I did was set a bedtime. Gone were the days of going to bed when I felt tired or when I was done watching a specific show. I could always think of one more thing to do, one more show in the series, one more social site to surf. If I was going to protect myself, then I needed to limit myself. I set a goal of eight hours of sleep.

When are we fully rested? Supposedly we're rested when we can wake up without using an alarm. I know this isn't always practical, but it's good to know. Taking care of our bodies is taking care of one of our most valuable possessions. Sleep is a sacred time. If we are to guard against the schemes of the enemy, we need to do everything in our power to protect our rest, to steward well this time to restart.

> GOD's loyal love couldn't have run out,
> his merciful love couldn't have dried up.

They're created new every morning.

How great your faithfulness! (Lam. 3:22–23)

I love this verse because sometimes I feel as though I've run out of grace. Of course, God's grace abounds, but I think some days need to end so we can begin again.

As a mother of four young children, I spend a portion of my time protecting their sleep as well. I also want to model healthy habits for them. If I know something is going to interrupt their sleeping patterns, I think long and hard about whether it's a necessary interruption. I want to set them up the best way I know how.

Also, it's vital for our kids to see that we are human beings with limits. Walking in to see Mom sitting down or Dad resting is important. Being a workaholic or being clinically exhausted isn't the best example for them. If we value sleep, they will too. We learn best when we see things modeled for us.

Let me say, there was a long season of my life when I was exhausted and couldn't remember the last time I'd slept through the night. I was either pregnant or nursing for almost five years. Ben had a part-time job that required him to get up three mornings a week at 3:30 a.m. by an alarm. He was burning the candle at both ends too. So if you're struggling, I get it. But a time will come when sleep needs to be a priority again. I want to keep that truth in front of you.

Date Nights and Sex Life

When I was a single woman, I always imagined I would love dating my husband. After all, I wouldn't be focusing so much on looking for the right guy as being with the right guy once I knew I had him. I imagined dressing up, picking a romantic restaurant, and running off to spend the evening together. Right? Wrong. Don't misunderstand me: I still love dating my husband, but it's a lot of effort to carve out the time and energy needed to make it happen.

Getting married is fun and being married is fun, but both require work. As every relationship needs work, marriage is no different. The beautiful part of marriage is that it was God's idea from the very beginning. He loves investing in and advocating for our lives together. He created what we call *covenant*. Simply put, a covenant is a commitment between a man and a woman under God for life. When we enter into covenant with another person, we then have access to anything they have access to. The same goes for our spouses. Anything available to us is available to them, both physically and spiritually. It's an incredible partnership.

Years ago I heard the Holy Spirit ask me to be more intentional about spending quality time with my husband. It's easy to be in the same room together, but it's another thing to share your dreams, your heart, and your vision. So we decided to establish a weekly date night. We begged, borrowed, and bartered for babysitting. Finding someone willing to watch our four young sons wasn't always easy, but we made it happen. Each week we'd plan everything, but without fail, sometime during the evening, I would hit my internal bedtime and continue the date delirious, exhausted, and a little embarrassed.

I finally looked at Ben on one of our dates and said,

"Look . . . I love having time with you. Date nights are one of my favorite things we do each week, but I can't enjoy them because I'm so sleepy. Would it be possible to do dates on Saturday mornings?"

He laughed, happily agreeing. It's painful for a young mom to try and stay awake or pay ten dollars to sleep through a movie. You know you've done it too!

After that, each Saturday morning, we'd run out, grab a coffee, and walk together. It wasn't sexy, but it was time— and that's what we needed. Inwardly I found a whole new peace in our relationship. I'll never forget the Holy Spirit speaking to me one morning after our time together. I heard him clearly say, "Your time with Ben is warfare. Each time you value what I value, it does damage to the enemy."

The enemy would love nothing more than to erode our relationships, specifically our marriages and covenant partnerships. Part of living stronger than the struggle is being intentional with those around us. I realize this isn't a book on marriage, but I want to share with you something I learned a few years ago that helped me. God made men and women for each other, and specifically, he made the act of sex. Yes, I know, we are going there—but just for a moment.

Sex is one of the most powerful weapons for the kingdom of God. Our enemy can't understand how two people can come together to create life. Satan is not God, so he is not a creator. Only God creates love, and only God creates humans. Only God creates the sanctity of connection and intimacy, giving us the ability to bond in a sovereign way. Satan can only counterfeit God's authentic plan.

Why create counterfeit sexuality and false intimacy? Pure intimacy is when you give your whole self—spirit, soul, and body—to someone else. When a man and a woman come together and are sexually intimate, it changes who they are and how they see themselves. It's precisely the reason why God designed sex. Sex is deeper than skin. Sex happens on a biological, psychological, and theological level.

God made the experience of sex to be between a husband and a wife. He created it to be so dynamic that the only safe place for its discovery was inside of marriage. God knew man and woman would know each other in a way no one else would know them, and he knew the power of fully knowing someone and being fully known. So he made marriage to protect the power of sex and that covenant with each other.

If we look deeper at the word *sex* in the Bible, we'll find its meaning goes as deeply as a form of worship. What happens between the sheets is worship. Ben and I like to say, "We were late because we were worshiping!" You'll get it later. In all seriousness, though, God sees marriage as sacred, and he created it to be enjoyable in every way.

Satan hates everything about these truths. He wants to abuse and pervert the very environment God created for us to help us bond and discover intimacy. That's why so many of our everyday battles have to do with marriage and relationships and intimacy.

What is one powerful way of doing warfare in this area? Go home and love your spouse. Spend time with him or her. Protect the potential cracks that leave room for the enemy. Build your life both spiritually and physically. Have fun! Enjoy each other. But most important, understand there is always more at stake than what you see. The enemy would love you to counterfeit everything God is trying to give you. Your marriage might be a fourteen-dollar day, but it's yours—and you've worked hard to have what you have. Don't be seduced by twenty-dollar moments. They cannot be sustained, and unreasonable expectations won't give you the fulfillment you might hope for.

Relationships are a risk. Marriage is a risk. A relationship you work to build for a lifetime, without fear of being replaced if you don't perform right, is a risk. But you are worth the risk!

Perfect and Good Enough

Mom guilt. I'd heard the term before but hadn't experienced it until I became a mom eleven years ago. I define *mom guilt* as a feeling of always being behind, imperfect, and lacking. I quickly learned to live with this negative feeling on a daily basis. I loved being a mom, but deep down I struggled to enjoy motherhood. I constantly wondered if I was doing something wrong or never doing enough.

The guilt persisted until I had a conversation with my mentor, who explained something that set me free. She said, "Havilah, you're going to have to stop being okay with only perfect and start being okay with good enough."

Confused, I asked her to explain.

She said that in life, we often have a picture in our minds of what perfect would contain. We quickly judge our outcome by measuring our real lives against our picture-perfect scenarios. Part of maturity, however—of growing and living in a whole space—is being able to look at something and being okay with the good-enough version: not defining *perfection* as success but being content with doing our very best.

Now let's be clear. I'm not suggesting we stop striving to grow and better steward our roles and responsibilities in life. This line of thought would be contrary to everything I live on a daily basis. What I am suggesting is acknowledging that most of us swing between states of perfectionism and performance. It doesn't always become evident when we have the time, money, or independence to make it happen. When we happen to become deficient in one area, our inner self can be overwhelmed by feelings of shame, guilt, and fear.

The enemy of our souls would love nothing more than to wear us out. He loves seeing us chase our tails. If he can get us to try a little harder, work a few more hours, take on just a bit more, he can motivate us into worshiping perfectionism and performance. Living in this space will always keep contentment a step out of reach.

Part of our defense is not to take ourselves so seriously that it robs us of enjoying the life Christ came to give us. Do we need to be diligent and determined? A resounding yes! But if we have an insatiable appetite for perfection at the cost of our mental, spiritual, and physical health, then we must evaluate the root of this inner desire and correct our course.

Celebrating Plus Ignoring

I had just finished preaching my fourth and final service of the weekend and was hurrying to jump in the car. Ben had left after the first service to load up our luggage and our boys, and now he had swung by to pick me up just as I finished. I looked around the car, and it was a familiar sight. I took off my heels and jewelry and managed to swig a drink of water. I was tired and looking forward to the long drive home.

After closing the door, I blurted out a familiar phrase. It was a mantra I said each time we ended a ministry trip: "Well, guys, let's ignore our losses and celebrate our successes!" The words were meant to remind me—really, to remind everyone in the car—that we were successful whether we believed it or not. We might have gotten called on a technical, but we played well and hard. That's what counts.

I can't tell you how much this truth has helped me through the years. My husband might chuckle each time I say my mantra out loud, but it's more for me than anyone. My ability to ignore my apparent lack and instead embrace the success of showing up has been crucial in my life. I'm not partnering with weakness, but I'm also not being defined by it. In each moment, each ministry trip, each book, and each message, there will be losses and wins. My responsibility is to focus on the successes, learn from the losses, but keep going no matter what.

Resilience is our secret spiritual weapon. It means the power or ability to return to the original form. When we experience hardships, trials, and tests, we have the Holy

Spirit inside of us encouraging us to come back to our original form. He reminds us of our identity in Christ. If there is one thing we can do to fight our enemy and win the struggle, it is to return to who we were created to be all along.

A couple of years ago, I was inspired to host a women's conference for our region. It was a massive undertaking, but I felt up to the challenge. I went to work building a team, inviting contributors, and asking our community to join me. After an incredible team effort, the event was a huge success. We sold out, making enough money to reinvest in the following year's event.

My team went back to work planning an identical event. Everything was moving forward just as before, but as we neared the time, our attendance estimates were much lower than anticipated. We worked hard promoting, but it just wasn't enough. We were short. By the time the event was over, we were $1,500 shy of the cost. There wasn't anything we could do.

I remember hearing the Holy Spirit encourage me that I had done my personal best. It was all he had asked of me. I had to make a decision that day: Was I going to celebrate my success or focus on the loss? We decided to go out for dinner the next night and celebrate, taking a moment to breathe in the goodness of God and all he had done in each woman's life.

The most amazing part of this story happened a couple of weeks later. I was talking with a mentor of mine and explaining how the event went when she asked point-blank, "Did you guys make your budget?" I responded by admitting we were $1,500 short but had decided to focus on all God had done. She responded, "You don't have to worry about that $1,500 anymore. I'm sending you a check today." I couldn't believe it. God had supplied all our needs. I'm confident God already knew what was going to happen, and my worry and fear would have been a waste of time.

Most of life is filled with fourteen-dollar moments, those pivotal places where we have a choice to make. We can spend our days focusing on our lack, the places that turned up empty. Or we can focus our full attention on celebrating our hard work and all God has done, coming to a place of celebration. Our effort is worthy, not because it is perfect but because we choose to show up. We live big. We take risks. We jump in the water with both feet!

EMPOWERMENT POINTS

- We only get distracted or feel cheated when we look at what others have received.
- Spiritual things look as practical as they do supernatural.
- Taking care of our bodies is taking care of one of our most valuable possessions.
- Each time you value what God values, it does damage to the enemy.
- Resilience is our secret spiritual weapon.

Chapter 12

Stronger Than the Struggle

I'm not sure what it is about children walking through the doors of stores, but the first thing they must do without fail is drink water and use the bathroom. It doesn't matter how many millions of times you've asked them to use the bathroom or drink water before leaving the house; when you walk into a store, their little bladders and dry mouths respond on cue. It's a fact.

This is how my kids are every time I walk into Target on my weekly pilgrimage. One particular day, though, I had a realization. I was inwardly grumbling as I grudgingly walked over to the drinking fountain, waiting for my older sons to drink so I could lift my littles up high enough for them to drink as well. After my oldest son had finished his five minutes of life-saving fluid intake, it was Hudson's turn.

Grayson had been watching the older boys take their time to drink and couldn't take it anymore. He passionately yelled, "Don't drink all of it!" and burst into tears. Grayson wasn't old enough to realize how the water fountain worked.

Hudson quickly responded to him, "Don't worry, Gray, it never runs out!"

Then I heard the Holy Spirit tell me, *Havilah, sometimes that's how you act too.* I knew what he was highlighting. Sometimes I overcomplicate what is already available to me. I make the dangerous assumption that if someone else is getting it, then of course I will be left wanting. I've found myself anxious about things like running out of time, getting lost in the journey, or fearing God's unquenchable love won't be enough for my debilitating earthly pain. My heart yells out, *Leave enough for me!* Then the Holy Spirit comes running to soothe the deepest parts of my heart, reminding me of my strength in him. There's always enough, but sometimes we don't act as though we believe it.

I once had a friend whose fiancé would humorously make her repeat after him: "I make a big deal out of small things, and it ruins our time together." We laughed as she told me about this ritual. But I have often thought of how guilty I am of this exact same thing.

Specifically, when it comes to my relationship with God, I tend to major in the minors. My focus gravitates to my mistakes and shortcomings, and I start to worry about how I measure up against everybody else and whether God will leave any blessing for my imperfect self. A mind-set like this traps us into performance and perfectionism before we know it, and we end up ignoring the important things—the call of God on our lives. Why do we do this? We fear our best won't be good enough, that if we reach for what God offers, we will expose our deepest fears of rejection and abandonment. So we don't reach at all, and we miss out on enjoying our time together.

Stronger Than the Struggle is my passionate pursuit to do the opposite of this, to reset our confused perspectives and help uncomplicate the spiritual battles we all face so we can walk freely and fully on the path God has laid out for us. It's about not making a big deal out of small things and ruining our time together with the Holy Spirit. It's about being well equipped for the big stuff in our spiritual lives, so we stay influential in our daily lives.

Is spiritual warfare a big subject? Yes. Can it feel overwhelming? Sometimes. But we remain overwhelmed when we either don't know where to start or don't think we have what it takes to get there.

Last year we purchased a new SUV we affectionately called "Our Fourth Bedroom." Most of the year we spend a lot of time driving, traveling, and camping, so it was worth the investment. We were thrilled to finally have all the bells and whistles a truck could provide; it was our dream come true. We quickly went into planning our summer, booking campsites, borrowing trailers, and asking for time off.

We were almost finished with our planning on the day Ben called me from work. I could hear the concern in his voice. "Honey, could you run out and look under the back bumper? Do you see a tow hitch?"

I jumped up and ran into the garage to look under the back bumper. I'm not much of a car girl, but I was sure I could spot a hitch. Well, you guessed it—there was nothing. No tow hitch. We were shocked. Ben suggested he call the dealer to see how much it would cost to put one on the car since most of our travels required one. Then he called back with bad news. It would cost us $1,100 to purchase and install our little hitch. We talked about adjusting our plans, canceling a few dates, and saving the money we now needed.

A few days later, Ben called me from work again, asking me to do the very same thing as before: look under the back bumper. I believe in miracles, but I hadn't ever thought of God giving us a tow hitch. Still, I was open. Ben, walking me through specific instructions, asked me to look for a panel on the back bumper. Finding it, I quickly pushed it open. Guess what was hiding under this pristine exterior? You guessed it. A tow hitch! Everything we needed to move forward. We laughed, thanking God we hadn't taken our car to the dealer and breathing a deep sigh of relief that we didn't have to spend the money.

Often, we can do the same thing. On first look, we may think we lack what we need, and we look for something everyone else seems to have already. But with a little more research and clarity, we will see we already have everything we need. Don't think for one moment you aren't well equipped for the battle. You have everything you need to thrive. Take a deep breath of relief. You are ready to go!

As we gear up to face the battles of life, I want to remind you of something we can't lose sight of: eternity.

> Fight the good fight of the faith [in the conflict with evil]; take hold of the eternal life to which you were called, and [for which] you made the good confession [of faith] in the presence of many witnesses. (1 Tim. 6:12 AMP)

Paul gave us direction when he told us to "fight the good fight of the faith," but the next line gives us our motivation. He said, "Take hold of the eternal life to which you were called." Having a clear idea of our destination will help us stay motivated in our spiritual battle. Eternity is waiting for us. Let's return to Ephesians one more time:

> And that about wraps it up. God is strong, and he wants you strong. So take everything the Master has set out for you, well-made weapons of the best materials. And put them to use, so you will be able to stand up to everything the Devil throws your way. This is no afternoon athletic contest that we'll walk away from and forget about in a couple of hours. This is for keeps, a life-or-death fight to the finish against the Devil and all his angels. (6:10–12)

We are amid a life-or-death fight, but it won't last forever. There will come a time, whether it's in heaven when we arrive or on earth when Christ returns, when the battle will end. Christ will have his reward. And this is what we fix our eyes on as we continue in our daily struggles: the hope of our future.

So, my friend, until we meet on earth or see each other in eternity, hold fast to truth and walk forward in the confidence that, because of Jesus, you really are stronger than the struggle.

Acknowledgments

Stronger than the Struggle is a compilation of twenty years of my life. Stories of victory and defeat, clarity and confidence, struggle and strength. But what you don't see in this book is the endless conversations, tears cried and long walks taken over the years, with my community of dear friends. These are my tribe. My people. The truth is, you wouldn't be holding this book without their love and influence in my life. Below is my best attempt to acknowledge my sincere and deepest gratitude.

Jessica Wong, Brigitta Nortker, and Stephanie Tresner, and the whole Thomas Nelson team: thank you for your diligent work on this book and editorial support. You gave me enough room to be myself and brought out the best of me for the world to see.

Thank you to my friend Rebekah Lyons for your generous forward and loving support. I knew we would be friends from the moment we crossed paths. Your books have been a life support to me.

To my friends who have invested their time and energy into this message: Jenn Johnson, Kris Vallotton, Bill Johnson, Heather Lindsey, Amanda Cook, Lisa Bevere, John Bevere, Bianca Olthoff, Lisa Harper, Christine Caine, Alli Worthington, Banning Liebscher, Shawn Bolz, Karen Wheaton, Real Talk Kim, and Charlotte Gambill. Thank you for practically showing me what the body of Christ looks like on a daily basis. You each inspire me!

Thank you to Ben, the love of my life (aka Babymaker). You are my hero, best friend, and partner in crime. You are the most exceptional and generous man I've ever known. Thank you for relentlessly loving me, standing behind me, and pushing me forward, even when I didn't think I had the strength to go on. I can only dream of what the future holds.

Mom and Dad, I hit the jackpot when it came to parents. Your unyielding pursuit to live authentic lives after Christ has been the propelling force behind my life. You called me a "leader" even as a little girl, speaking this truth until it became a reality. I'm forever grateful. Deborah, my wombmate and best friend, thank you for being a perpetual source of wisdom, intuition, and laughter. You and Daniel are one of the greatest gifts to my life.

Friends who have become family—Mike, Dawn, Jen, and Tony, (and hopefully the marriage of our kids "wink"). Jerry, Staci, Tim, Rach, Wes, and Matt, let's spend more time in the Jacuzzi. Jamie and Sarah, maybe one day we'll live by each other on the beach.

Kris Vallotton, you never looked at my full life as a limitation but believed in me and invested in me. I'm forever grateful for you and Kathy's belief in our family. We will be friends for life!

Thank you, Tiffany Cochran, for being a vital part of my life. You have been a voice of unlimited encouragement, counsel, and love. You took me more seriously than I took myself. You are a rare find!

In 2015 God brought FOUR Lisa's in my life that changed the entire trajectory of my life:

Lisa Bevere, you were the friend, mentor, and Italian godmother I desperately needed in my life. Only God knows how deep my love runs for you. You are my person. Let's spend the next twenty years laughing about our man cubs and our crazy, naked, lives.

Lisa Harper, you are the only reason this book happened. You introduced me to your agent, Lisa Jackson and the reassurance that I could do it. Thank you for making me laugh! You're good for the soul.

Lisa Jackson and the whole Alive Agency, thank you for holding my hand through the unknown waters of publishing. Your constant belief, encouragement, and calming voice have been my confidence on the other side of the phone. Let's dream again!

Lysa Terkeurst, I'll never forget the moment we met and I asked you what you did, and you said, "I write books." I asked, "What's the book called?" OMG. Realizing your legendry gift, my embarrassment quickly developed into a deep love for you. I asked you every question I could about writing books, and you graciously answered each one. I treasured those moments.

Bethel Church, you are the most amazing community. Your quest to live out the words of Jesus is your greatest strength. You truly are some of the best on the planet. History will tell the true story of sacrifice you've each made!

To the women in my life (aka Girl Gang), Michelle, Renee, Danielle, Lauren, and Jenna, thank you for making me feel normal.

To the women who made me believe strong is not wrong—Joyce Meyer, Beth Moore, Oprah, Dr. Laura, Lisa Bevere, Christine Caine, Bianca Olthoff, Susan Schmit, Suzie Anfuso, Beni Johnson, Donna Desilva, Dr. Anne Marie Adams, Joelle Morgan, Kathy Cannon, Sarah Pridgen, Staci Schilz, Robyn Niles, Lesley Crandall, Stephanie Brubaker, Holly Brunson, Suzanne Ecker, Andi Andrews, and so many more I'm sure I'll remember right after I send this to the publisher.

To all those who have supported me over the years, I may not know your name, but I feel your love on a daily basis. You've bought my books, shared my posts, and joined my table at Truth to Table. Thank you for being my colaborers. I hope my ceiling becomes your floor.

Lastly, but certainly the most important relationship in my life, Jesus Christ my Lord and Savior. Thank you for creating me, loving me, and leading me in this life. I can't wait to spend eternity together!

About the Author

Havilah Cunnington has been in full-time ministry for twenty years, which has taken her throughout the world. She serves as the executive director of Moral Revolution and a pastor at Bethel Church. Recently Havilah and her husband, Ben, began a nonprofit and an online platform called Truth to Table. Their desire is to reach the world around them from their kitchen table with Bible studies, messages, and lifestyle leadership tools. Havilah and Ben reside in Redding, California, with their four sons: Judah, Hudson, Grayson, and Beckham.

Notes

Chapter 1: Spiritual Warfare in Real Life

1. Oswald Chambers, "Let Us Keep to the Point," *My Utmost for His Highest*, January 1, 2017, https://utmost.org/classic/let-us-keep-to-the-point-classic.
2. Chris Durso, Twitter post, December 6, 2016, https://twitter.com/ChrisDurso.
3. David Guzik, "Study Guide for James 1," *Blue Letter Bible*, 2007, https://www.blueletterbible.org/Comm/guzik_david/StudyGuide_Jam/Jam_1.cfm.

Chapter 2: Two Camps

1. Joseph LeDoux, "Rethinking the Emotional Brain," *Neuron* 73, no. 4 (February 2012): 653–76.
2. Caroline Webb, *How to Have a Good Day: Harness the Power of Behavioral Science to Transform Your Working Life* (New York: Crown, 2016).
3. Ibid., 25.

4. Rick Renner, *Sparkling Gems from the Greek* (Tulsa, OK: Teach All Nations, 2003), 942.

Chapter 3: A Fight Worth Fighting
1. John Wooden, *They Call Me Coach* (New York: McGraw Hill, 2004), 85.

Chapter 4: An Angel with a God Complex
1. T. D. Jakes, Twitter post, November 30, 2012, https://twitter.com/BishopJakes.
2. Rick Renner, *Sparkling Gems from the Greek 2* (Tulsa, OK: Harrison House, 2016), 125.
3. Rick Renner, *Sparkling Gems from the Greek* (Tulsa, OK: Teach All Nations, 2003), 604.

Chapter 6: Satan Comes to Kill
1. Rick Renner, *Sparkling Gems from the Greek* (Tulsa, OK: Teach All Nations, 2003), 547.
2. Dawna De Silva, Facebook post, November 13, 2015, https://www.facebook.com/dawna.desilva.

Chapter 7: Satan Comes to Destroy
1. Rick Renner, *Sparkling Gems from the Greek* (Tulsa, OK: Teach All Nations, 2003), 395.

Chapter 8: Know the Word
1. Flavius Vegetius Renatus, *The Military Institutions of the Romans*, trans. John Clarke (Los Angeles: Enhanced Media, 2017), 13–14.

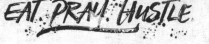

DISCOVER HOW TO HEAR
GOD'S VOICE IN YOUR EVERYDAY LIFE

JOIN OUR EMPOWERMENT COURSE:

Prophetic Personalities

8 VIDEO LESONS

Drawing from years of experience, Havilah Cunnington will teach on four types of prophetic gifts, unleashing you into a bold life of hearing from Heaven.

8 ACTIVATIONS

Weekly challenges where you can put into practice what you've learned.

8 ENCOURAGEMENTS

Coaching from Havilah on how to follow through in your pursuit to hear God in new ways.

&

DOWNLOADABLE WORKSHEETS

ADDED BONUSES

TRUTH to TABLE
TRUTHTOTABLE.COM